Feb. 25th, 2020

To Beck

I pr[...]
You to be a mighty prayer warrior
and witness for the gospel of christ
like Patrick!

Jessica Dunn

PATRICK
A SPARK IN THE DARKNESS

JESSICA DUNN

LifeRich Publishing is a registered trademark of
The Reader's Digest Association, Inc.

LifeRich Publishing books may be ordered through booksellers or by contacting:

LifeRich Publishing
1663 Liberty Drive
Bloomington, IN 47403
www.liferichpublishing.com
1 (888) 238-8637

Because of the dynamic nature of the Internet, any web addresses or
links contained in this book may have changed since publication and
may no longer be valid. The views expressed in this work are solely those
of the author and do not necessarily reflect the views of the publisher,
and the publisher hereby disclaims any responsibility for them.

Any people depicted in stock imagery provided by Getty Images are
models, and such images are being used for illustrative purposes only.
Certain stock imagery © Getty Images.

Illustrations by Joshua Dunn
Front cover design by Lydia Zach

ISBN: 978-1-4897-2651-3 (sc)
ISBN: 978-1-4897-2652-0 (e)

Print information available on the last page.

LifeRich Publishing rev. date: 01/27/2020

Contents

Acknowledgements

First, I am grateful to my husband Mark for encouraging me to write this book and get it published, as well as helping me with research at the very beginning of this project and providing endless encouragement to keep writing. Your confidence in me kept me going! Many thanks to my son Joshua for creating the amazing illustrations. Thank you to my sons Joshua, Timothy, and Benjamin for listening to me read excerpts to them, and for their patience in allowing me the time to write. Heartfelt thanks to Laura Miller for her time, expertise, and thoroughness in editing this book, and for her advice and insight on many details. Many thanks to Lydia Zach for designing the front cover. Thank you to all my family and friends who prayed for me and encouraged me as I struggled to bring this book to completion. Lastly, I want to thank all the kids (and grown-ups) who will read this book. May you come to know who Patrick truly was, and may you know the power of the gospel in your life as Patrick did.

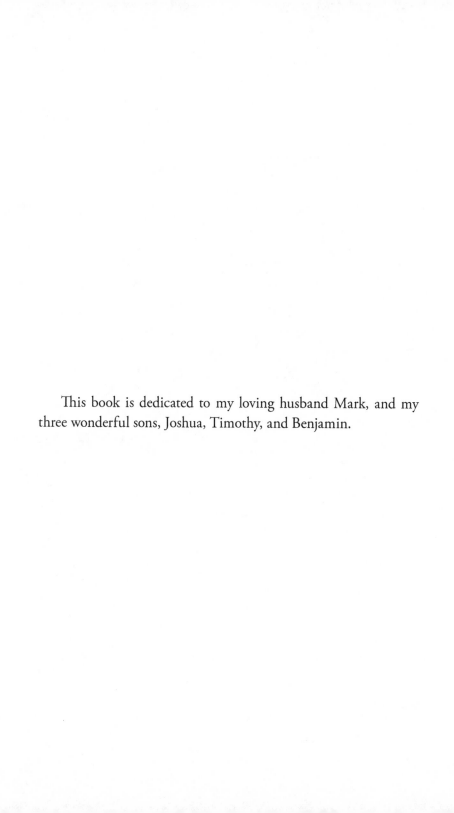

This book is dedicated to my loving husband Mark, and my three wonderful sons, Joshua, Timothy, and Benjamin.

Prologue

The year was 387, Britain. A beam of light pierced through the window of the ancient church and rested upon the new-born infant cradled in the priest's arms. The baby's cries echoed throughout the still church as a trickle of water slid down the side of his face. The priest chanted the familiar words, "Patricius Magonus Sucatus, I baptize you in the name of the Father, the Son, and the Holy Ghost." After a prayer of dedication, the priest handed the baby back to his father.

Calpurnius looked down into the tiny, bright eyes. He had high hopes for his son. One day he would inherit everything he had worked for. All his time and energy would go into making a grand life for this little one.

Chapter 1

Bannavem

The glow of the fire was welcome company that evening as Patrick and Lupita sat playing Tabula Lusoria. Patrick watched Lupita, his older sister by two years, place three counters on the edge of the circle. She always won, managing to get three in a row. Patrick was determined to win this time. But again he was unsuccessful.

"Let's play knucklebones now," Patrick demanded as he grabbed his set from the satchel where he had been hiding them. He threw them up into the air and caught them on the back of his hand with a squeal of delight.

"I got one dog, one Vulcan, one eagle, and one Caesar," Patrick taunted his sister. "You try."

He watched as Lupita threw them up into the air and then laughed when all her bones fell to the floor.

"Where did you get those?" Patrick's grandfather curiously interrupted.

"My friend Flavius gave them to me," Patrick commented. "All the kids are playing this. It's fun."

Patrick didn't notice as his grandfather and mother exchanged concerned glances. Putting down the book he was reading, Potitus thought quietly for a moment and then asked his grandson, "Why don't you go over the Apostle's Creed for me?"

"Aw, I did that last night," complained Patrick.

"Patrick, do as your grandfather says," his mother chided, attempting to go back to her piecework.

With a sullen voice Patrick began reciting, "I believe in God the Father Almighty, Maker of heaven and earth, and in Jesus Christ his only begotten Son, . . . " He finished, looking over at his grandfather, knowing he wasn't pleased.

"Alright, time for bed, you two," Patrick's mother spoke up. "You have school in the morning, Patrick."

Grudgingly, Patrick and Lupita hastened off to their bedrooms.

The sunlight pouring into the window of the school was so welcome after the many days of gloomy drizzle.

"Why do I have to be stuck in here learning Latin," thought Patrick, "when there is a little bit of sun outside?" He had been at school since just after dawn.

The magister, seeing the frustration on his pupils' faces, pushed them even harder. "Pay attention to me, not outside!" he spoke sternly as he walked around the room of boys. The methodical tap of his pointer on the tiled floor kept in sync with the tempo of voices chanting declensions in unison. After another half hour of monotonous reciting, he dismissed the small class of boys.

Patrick picked up his wax tablet and stylus, left the school building and ran through the forum of Bannavem to find his friend Flavius.

The town of Bannavem lay on top of a hill that rose up off the western coast of Britain. Over on top a nearby hill, at the head of the valley, Patrick could barely make out the standing stones where the ancestors of Bannavem used to gather.

The market was bustling with people getting ready for Christmas. Patrick meandered through the covered portico and along the rows of small shops. He ran in and out through the colonnades where the merchants were busy selling their goods. Patrick spotted one of his father's servants buying ale. A busy merchant used an abacus to make calculations for prices.

Patrick then passed the basilica, a great hall where public meetings took place and laws were passed by the council. His father, Calpurnius, was a Decurion, an office held only by wealthy citizens. Calpurnius had to attend many long meetings at the basilica.

Stopping to glance cautiously around him, Patrick looked toward the back of the basilica. His mother and grandfather did not like him peering into these rooms. Patrick couldn't help being curious about them, though. He even went into them once. In the center was the shrine to Aedes. There was a statue of the emperor and statues of important Roman gods and goddesses. The Romans had so many gods. Flavius had told Patrick about how he would go there with his father to pray to the gods. He couldn't help wondering how his grandfather was so certain that there was only one true God. Since the Romans had brought so much good to Bannavem, why were their gods not good, too?

Patrick spied Flavius walking along the ramparts near the guard tower. Flavius's father was a soldier in the Roman army stationed in Bannavem. The boys liked to walk and play along the ramparts, pretending they were soldiers.

"So, are you coming with me to the festival?" Flavius asked as he swept dark hair out of his eyes.

"Of course," said Patrick. "I just have to come up with a way to get out without my mother and grandfather knowing."

"You won't get caught," Flavius countered. Your family will be so busy with their own Christmas celebrations."

The two boys walked past a shrine to a Roman god and then stopped at the beginning of the lane that led to Patrick's family villa, just outside Bannavem.

"It's going to be so much fun. Everyone is going to be there. I'll meet you at my father's quarters."

Patrick left Flavius and meandered slowly along the long, well-worn path. He passed the many graves of the dead, many of whom had died in the battles against the Picts and Scots. Patrick found his thoughts dwelling on the Romans who came and drove all the invaders away. The citizens of Bannavem were proud to be Roman. Rome ruled the world. Rome brought civilization to Britain. And Rome brought protection and security to his quiet, little village. "I can't understand why being friends with Flavius is such a bad idea," Patrick mused. "The festival Flavius was going to sounded like so much fun, a lot more fun than sitting around at home listening to grown-ups talk."

As he got near to his father's villa, Patrick paused to watch his father's slaves working in the fields. He could see the Irish Sea stretched out below. In the distance, at the edge of the world, Patrick could make out the mysterious land called Ireland, where the dreaded barbarians lived.

"I'm glad I am Roman and not one of those barbarians," Patrick thought to himself. "And I'm certainly glad I'm not a slave."

The sun was shining, reflecting off the clay tiled roof of the family villa. Seven speckled hens were scratching in the dirt, looking for bugs. Patrick's mother, Conchessa, met him in the courtyard. Her long tunic flowed behind her, her stola belted at her thin waist. She had her wool cloak drawn tightly around her.

"Succat, you're home early."

"The magister let us out," Patrick answered.

"Were you spending time with that soldier's son?" Conchessa asked in an accusing tone. "You have, haven't you?"

Patrick cringed. He hated his mother calling him Succat. It wasn't Roman. She always called him that when she wasn't happy with him. "Here I go again having to defend my friendship with Flavius," Patrick sighed to himself. "I . . . it's hard to not . . ." Patrick tried to reply.

"Flavius is not good company, Succat," Conchessa went on. "Stay away from Flavius. Do you understand?"

"Yes, mother," Patrick replied, spying the servant he had seen in the market buying ale.

Conchessa hurried back into the villa, yelling orders to servants. Patrick walked over to the storage shed where the young slave was unloading the ale from a cart.

"You good for nothing slave!" Patrick roared at the quivering young man. "Why do you care who I hang out with? If you get me into trouble again, I'll tell my father!"

Patrick headed to the stables hoping to find his father. What was so bad about hanging around Flavius, anyway? he wondered. He could always count on his father to take his side. When his grandfather or mother tried to set unfair rules or get him to do something he didn't want to do, his father usually intervened for him.

Calpurnius was a strong, successful, wealthy man. He didn't pray to God. He did what he wanted, and things seemed to work out for him. He never seemed worried about what he did or who he spent time with.

The sound of loud baying told Patrick his father had just come back from a hunt. The hounds were scampering around excitedly.

"Dismissed early?" Calpurnius asked his son. "Then why do you look so gloomy?"

Patrick recounted the conversation with his mother.

"Don't let your mother and grandfather get you down, Patrick. I'm sure Flavius is a good friend. I know his father. He lost some money to me on the races!" Calpurnius laughed and handed the horse's reigns to a servant.

Feeling a little better, Patrick left the stables. He crossed through the courtyard and over the broad mosaic floor of the living room. Patrick always marvelled at the tiny specks of blue, red, and yellow colored clay that made up the huge picture of the country scene beneath him.

In his bedroom Patrick found his clean, new toga laid out upon his bed. He could hear the household servants preparing for the Christmas banquet his parents were hosting the following day. He picked up the carving he was working on. The sheep bone felt smooth in his hand. His small knife easily made impressions into the soft bone as he put the last touches on a hunting dog. Setting the bone down, Patrick wondered how he would be able to slip out of the house tomorrow and go to the festival with Flavius.

That evening Patrick sat on a hard, wooden pew in the church where his grandfather was a priest. The service rambled on in Latin. His grandfather stood behind the altar in the apse, a small semi-circular area. His mind carelessly wandered away from him. He knew his grandfather had high hopes of him becoming a priest in the future.

"This is so boring," he thought. "There is no way I am ever going to be a priest."

Patrick sensed his grandfather looking at him and made a half-hearted attempt to pay attention.

"I don't understand why I have to be here," he thought. "Especially since I'm never becoming a priest. I will take over my father's estate when I am older. Then I will be able to do what I want. I won't have anyone telling me what to do. I'll be in control and will be one of the most powerful decurions in Britain! And I won't ever have to come to church again!"

Patrick looked at the purple sash on his father's toga, symbolizing his position as Decurion. "Why would I give up everything to become some weak, poor priest?" he thought.

Patrick felt the coin he held in his hand. There was a picture of the emperor wearing a crown, with the inscription *Sol Invictus*, "to the Unconquered Sun". Sol was the official sun god of the Roman Empire and the patron god of soldiers.

While Patrick and his family were celebrating Christmas, the birth of Jesus Christ, Flavius and his father, with the whole Roman army, would be celebrating the festival of Sol Invictus tomorrow, the birth of the sun.

"How would it look, a Decurion's son, a priest's grandson, taking part in a pagan festival?" Patrick could hear his grandfather asking him.

Chapter 2

Christmas

Christmas morning found Patrick accompanying his grandfather to Bannavem. Their first stop was the baths.

Patrick winced as the strigil scraped the skin on his back. The only reason he endured this treatment was because he was able to have a warm bath afterwards in the tepidarium. The slave assigned to clean Patrick's skin today seemed heavy handed.

Patrick looked over at his grandfather, who seemed to be enjoying his cleaning. Potitus came to the baths often, taking the opportunity to talk with whoever he met. He was always talking about God.

"Cleaning the body is good for you, Patrick," his grandfather said warmly. "It reminds us how we need cleansed by Jesus. We have so much filth in our lives."

"Yes, grandfather, I know." Patrick loved spending time with his grandfather at the baths but felt embarrassed when he started his lecturing about Jesus. There were many times when Patrick could overhear others making fun of his grandfather, mimicking him as he talked.

The two finally made their way to the tepidarium. The warm water relaxed Patrick. Thankfully, because of Christmas and the festival, there weren't too many people using the baths today. Everyone was getting ready for the festivities.

"Patrick, I am concerned for you," Potitus said in a low voice. "I pray for you to trust God, to trust in Christ." Potitus stifled a cough. "You know I say these things because I love you."

"You don't have to worry about me, grandfather. I'm fine." Patrick felt bad he caused his grandfather to worry on his account. "I know God is with me," he said as he managed a smile.

"Patrick, if you do not trust Christ, there will be terrible consequences for you. I pray that you will believe."

"I do believe in God," Patrick defended himself.

"Your mother and I are worried you are spending too much time with this new friend of yours," Potitus said.

"You mean Flavius?" Patrick questioned. "What's so bad about him? His father is a Roman soldier!"

"Flavius does not believe in the one true God, Patrick. You must be careful with whom you spend your time. Even friends can lead you astray, and into wrong."

"I've heard father say that Rome has brought only good to Britain."

Patrick and Potitus stepped out of the water. Next a masseur rubbed them down with smelling oils and scents.

After putting on their togas, grandfather and grandson walked out of the baths and into the hustle and bustle of Bannavem. They completed some errands and found the road that led to their villa. As they walked on in silence Patrick wondered why his grandfather was so hard on him. Didn't his grandfather know that he believed in God? But Patrick wasn't certain there was only one true God. Patrick respected and loved his grandfather, but he wasn't too sure about his views on things. Praying was okay for older people. But why bother to spend time praying when you are young and strong?

The villa was busy with preparations for the Christmas banquet. The servants in the kitchen were busy cooking Patrick's favorite, suckling pig, which was boiled in milk. The aroma of freshly baked bread found its way to Patrick's nostrils, making his mouth water.

He could hear his parents in the reception room talking with some fellow decurions and their wives. Patrick ventured into the dining room where the table was laid with all the fanciest dishes in the villa. He always admired the hunting scenes that were etched onto the pots.

Hardly able to contain his excitement, not only for the feast, but for what he was scheming to do later, Patrick busied himself with sneaking samples of food from the dishes. Lupita entered the dining room adorning her new, golden torc around her neck. Her mother had given the necklace to her as an early Christmas present. She was admired by all the company as they gathered for the feast.

After a prayer from his grandfather, the feasting began. Patrick stuffed his face till he could eat no more. He watched his father's jolly antics, fuelled by the decurions' bellowing laughter as Calpurnius retold the story of his hunt yesterday. Lupita, his mother, and the other ladies were talking the quick, quiet talk that ladies talk when they want no one else to hear. The servant who told on Patrick came in to pour more ale. Patrick glared at him, still seething for what he had done.

"I can't wait to get away," Patrick thought to himself.

His grandfather had already removed himself from the scene and had retired to his room to rest. The servants had cleared the dishes and were now in their own small dining room eating their own feast.

Calpurnius got up and invited the men to the stables. He wanted to show off his hunting dogs.

"Patrick, you come too," Calpurnius said.

Patrick quickly jumped out of his seat, glad of the opportunity to leave the table. This was his way out. His nervous energy made it impossible to sit there any longer.

The dogs were Calpurnius's pride and joy. As the group neared the stables Patrick could hear the baying of the hounds. His father threw the bones left over from the feast to the dogs. Once inside the wooden structure, Calpurnius motioned for Patrick to come over to him as he unlatched a waddle gate. Bounding out was the most beautiful hound dog Patrick had ever seen. He had a sleek grey coat and eyes of coal.

"Happy Christmas, son!" Calpurnius said, smiling down at Patrick. The dog began sniffing Patrick excitedly with his black nose.

"Thank you, Father!" Patrick said as he knelt to pet his very own hunting dog. "I've already got the perfect name for him. Maxi! Can I take him out?"

"Sure, of course," Calpurnius said approvingly. "Just make sure your home before dark."

Chapter 3

Sol Invictus

With Maxi scampering along at his side, Patrick headed down the lane toward Bannavem. He couldn't wait to show Flavius his new dog. Patrick immediately felt relief in each step as the excitement of what he was about to do propelled him toward the town. He pulled his cucullus over his head for warmth, feeling the wind coming in from the Irish Sea.

Patrick spied Flavius and his father over at the gaming counters.

"Nice dog," Flavius said, admiring the companion at Patrick's side. "Come on, let's go have some fun." The two boys made their way through the crowds as Patrick told Flavius his tale of how he had gotten away.

They first made their way to the temple. There was a great crowd assembled eager for the festivities to begin. The pontifice, priest to the sun god, stood in front of an altar. Images of the sun and moon were seen on an altar of glass in the temple. There was a dished area on the top of the altar known as the focus. A fire of pinecones was burning, sending pleasant smelling fragrances to the noses of the attenders, meant to attract the attention of the gods. A ram was brought forth by two soldiers. To Patrick's surprise the pontifice unsheathed a jewel studded dagger and slit the ram's throat, slaughtering it as a sacrifice to the gods. Both in horror and curious fascination, Patrick watched the ram slump to the ground as its life fleeted out of its body. A haruspex, or prophet, came forward and inspected the innards of the ram, to tell the future. Flavius said that the haruspex would know if the soldiers were going to have good fortune in battle. Patrick waited with anticipation for what was going to happen next. This was so much more interesting than sitting in a boring church listening to a priest rambling on in Latin.

Patrick and Flavius then joined the throng headed to the hill with the standing stones for the games held in honor of the sun god. Flavius grabbed Patrick's hand and led him to a group of people who had formed a circle. The circle of people danced around and around in honor of the sun. Not knowing the words, Patrick listened to the people chant the Druid song, *Leabhar breac,* Ode to the Sun.

"O Sun! thou mighty Lord of the heavens, sole and general God of man, thou gracious, just, and supreme King, to whom heroes pray in perils of war, all the world praises and adores thee."

Dizzy with dancing, Patrick was then moved with the crowd to where a huge bonfire was lit in an open field. A gigantic circle big enough to hold a mob of people was cut out on the turf, with the fire lit inside. The throng of people continued to dance around the fire, waving torches around their heads in a sunward direction. Patrick watched as the young soldiers leaped through the flames and glowing embers.

"Isn't this fun?" Flavius questioned Patrick.

Patrick couldn't remember having so much fun. He kept looking over to the edge of the field where he had tied Maxi to a tree. Seeing him there, Patrick resumed dancing. High on adrenaline from the rush of the dancing, he let himself loose, enjoying every minute of it. He felt so free. No one was there to tell him what to do. What was so wrong with this, anyway? Didn't God want people to have fun? He wasn't hurting anyone.

Finally wiped out from all the frenzy, Patrick and Flavius sat in the shade where Maxi was left. They hungrily ate at the cakes given to each of them. The cakes were made of oatmeal, eggs and milk, and were baked in the bonfire.

The two boys watched as the chosen boy, the boy who got the cake daubed with the black embers, was blindfolded and had to leap through the flames three times.

"That boy pulled out the blackened piece," explained Flavius. "He is chosen as the devoted person, the victim to be sacrificed to obtain good luck for the year. Bel, the Sun god will now give us good luck."

Patrick headed back to his villa happy and, for the first time in a long time, feeling content and sure of himself. Today had been a good day. He looked down at his new dog, Maxi, loyally trotting along by his side, sniffing at the wind.

By the time he returned to the villa his mother, grandfather, and sister were sound asleep. There was no sign of his father. He was probably in the stables, or could be in Bannavem, gambling and drunk.

Chapter 4

The Roman Army Leaves

Seeing his grandfather the following morning made Patrick feel a little guilty about what he had participated in. He knew that his grandfather would be deeply disappointed in him, and even very upset, if he found out.

But the news his grandfather had to share with him made the worry of yesterday's sin seem minor.

"Patrick, I have something I need to talk with you about," Potitus said while sitting near the fire in the living room.

Patrick could see in his grandfather's eyes that something was troubling him deeply. He sat on the ground next to him, and Maxi, stretching out his long legs, lay down beside him. For a minute, Patrick worried that he had been found out about yesterday. But how could his grandfather know? Patrick remembered the ale servant. But he couldn't know. The slave would have been caught up in all the cleaning up of yesterday's feast.

"Patrick, your father rode into Bannavem early this morning.

Word came yesterday concerning the Roman army. They are leaving Bannavem."

"What? Why?" Patrick stammered, trying to take in all that this meant.

"The emperor has ordered the army to leave Britain and return to Italy. Rome is under attack, Patrick."

Potitus watched his troubled grandson run out of the room, Maxi following close after his master. Potitus's heart ran after Patrick, wanting to console him and give further explanation. Potitus grieved for his grandson. He knew the army leaving would be a big blow to Patrick and to all in Bannavem. But Potitus worried what this might do to Patrick's soul. There would be no more Flavius to influence him, but would this drive him farther from knowing the one true God?

Patrick stood outside the barracks and watched the columns of soldiers marching by. The centurion at the head of the legion rode on a majestic white stallion. As Patrick watched them leave, he felt his security and peace leave with them.

Calpurnius stood beside his son, watching the soldiers march down the main street of Bannavem.

"I thought they would be able to stay here in Britain forever," Patrick said to his father.

"The Vandals have attacked Italy, and Emperor Honorius has called all his forces to return. Flavius's father's battalion leaves in the morning."

Patrick stood beside his father speechless. The entire Roman army in Britain would be leaving. Flavius might even be leaving. Suddenly Bannaven seemed very empty and vulnerable. All the happiness Patrick had felt suddenly left him like a mighty wind blowing through him.

Patrick climbed to the top of the hill behind the villa, Maxi at his side. His world was falling apart. The soldiers were leaving. Flavius would probably be leaving. What would be next? He stood there for what seemed like an eternity, listening to the waves crashing on the shore.

"Trust God. He is always in control." That is what his grandfather would say.

Patrick wasn't so sure. Where was God in all this? God seemed so very far away. How could he trust in someone he couldn't see?

Patrick lay in bed that night thinking. He could hear his parents talking with his grandfather in the room below him.

"What are we going to do?" Patrick's mother asked. "We can't leave Succat here alone anymore now that the army is leaving."

"I know, Conchessa," said Calpurnius. "With the army gone, Britain will be left open for invaders. Greece has already been laid waste by the Goths. Athens was completely destroyed by them."

"It's the Irish we should be concerned about!" said Potitus. "If only Emperor Theodosius were still alive. He would never have allowed this to happen."

"Emperor Honorius is too weak, sleeping while King Alaric and his army are on the attack," replied Calpurnius. "In town today, the other decurions and I had a meeting. We will be responsible for the safety and defence of Bannavem now. Rome will no longer give us safety. Hadrians's wall will probably never be rebuilt now."

Patrick felt a shiver run down his spine. He had heard his grandfather tell stories of Irish raiders who came across the sea to Britain to capture and plunder.

The next morning Patrick stood out at the edge of his father's field, looking out over the sea. He had never thought much about the Irish before, those wild savages who lived at the end of the earth. But now they seemed so close he could reach out and touch them. He turned his gaze to his father's flock of sheep grazing in the field, and watched the slave tending to them. At least if raiders did come, they would go for the slaves first, thought Patrick. The slaves' quarters were located outside near the family's villa, facing the sea.

Chapter 5

Kidnapped!

Across the Irish sea, in the land known as the end of the world, King Niall, high king of Ireland, sat on his throne in his hall. The time had now come. His men were ready. Tonight they would go.

King Niall motioned to one of his warriors. "Fachmad, get yourself and your men ready. You leave tonight." The raiders grabbed their weapons, and with a shout to their king, they thundered out of the hall.

The boats full of Irish warriors eager for plunder pushed off into the darkness and made their way to Britain. After a long night they slipped up to the shore. The little town of Bannavem lay peaceful in the moonlight, unaware of the raiders running deftly toward it.

Unprepared, the sleeping citizens were helpless against the vicious attack. Plundering and capturing as they went, the raiders swept through the village, wanting to load their vessels with as much treasure and captives as they could.

Everyone in Patrick's villa was sound asleep. Even Maxi lay asleep on the floor at the side of Patrick's bed. But Patrick lay awake thinking. All he could think about were the rows of Roman soldiers marching out of the village. Flavius had left as well, to go back to

Italy with his father. The world as he knew it was changing so fast. The village was ripe with fear. Now that the Roman soldiers were gone, Britain was open to barbarians and, even closer to home, raiders from Ireland.

This wasn't the first time his parents were away from the villa, but with the Romans gone, things were different. Patrick felt afraid. He had often been found gazing out across the Irish Sea toward that savage land. It seemed closer now than ever.

Patrick kept thinking about his grandfather's words to him. "We must trust in God," he would say. As hard as he wanted to please his grandfather, Patrick could not bring himself to trust in his God. He knew it caused his grandfather much grief and worry, and he felt terrible about that, too.

As Patrick finally drifted off to sleep, the band of Irish raiders was quietly finding their way along the path leading to Patrick's villa.

Suddenly, Maxi sprang up, his ears pricked to full attention. Patrick had no time to fight back. He woke to barbarians entering his room and throwing him on the ground. They gagged him and bound his hands painfully behind his back. Too frightened to resist, Patrick was marched downstairs. Horror and grief seized him as he watched his grandfather and older slaves slaughtered in front of him. A chain was fastened around his neck, and along with some of the villa's younger and fitter servants, he was marched off in line to the waiting boats. He caught sight of Lupita bound in the same manner, chained along with female slaves. She was wailing frantically. Patrick was too numb to even cry out to her.

Patrick sat in shock in the rocking boat. Three feet of iron links separated him from the next captive. He didn't even notice that the body connected to him by the chain of iron was the hated ale slave. A dawning realization was slowly coming to Patrick that his life had suddenly, horribly changed forever—and not for the better.

But little did the pagan raiders know, as they headed home, was that their brutal activities that day would change the history of their island forever.

Chapter 6

Now a Slave

King Niall sat at the head of the table in his great hall, feasting and celebrating the successful return of his raiders. The nobles and druids had come to listen to the reports of the raiding parties. All the plunder of the recent raid was lavishly displayed before them. Treasures taken from homes were pawed through, and the people so violently abducted were huddled together along one of the walls.

Patrick, starving and cold, sat chained to a pole in a corner of the hall, the ale slave still attached to him. Tomorrow he would be sold. He knew slaves were very valuable from the amount of money his father had spent on them. Patrick was able to learn what was happening from the Irish slaves captured from Bannavem.

"Sing to us, bard, about the great raid on Britain," King Niall bellowed. The Irish warriors raised their voices in a thunderous cheer as the bard started singing a song about the great raid that destroyed Patrick's life.

There was no hope of rescue. Patrick was now prisoner on the wild island that was beyond the reach of civilized Britain. There was no Roman army to come after him. The Roman Empire was the world, and now he was outside it.

"God has definitely left me," Patrick thought. "Was there even a God? Why should I love a God who would allow this to happen to me?" Patrick didn't know what to think anymore. He couldn't think. "Why did believing in God matter now?" All he needed to do now was to survive. And he wasn't sure he even wanted to do that.

Over and over in his mind Patrick kept seeing his grandfather killed before his eyes. He had not seen Lupita since that awful day they were both taken so viciously away from their home. He had heard that the female captives were being taken to an area called Louth to be sold. "Where was Louth? Was it nearby? Will I see my sister again?" Patrick wondered.

"Disgusting," Patrick thought, thinking of his beautiful, elegant sister being sold for the equivalent of three milk cows. He had never felt such hatred before. He hated the Irish. And if there was a God, he hated him, too.

Patrick and a few other captives had been carried north until they arrived in Antrim. He now sat in the dirt, chained to another pole, still attached to the ale slave. He had been poked and prodded by all the men of the tuath. His once beautiful, white toga had been ripped off him and replaced with a ragged cloth that was now torn and filthy. The dirt was now turning to mud as the rain turned heavier.

"I hate this place and I hate the Irish!" Patrick wailed, pitying himself.

A young man approached the two captives. Patrick remembered seeing the man earlier. He was tall and muscular and had dark brown hair that trailed down to his shoulders. The man pulled on Patrick's arm, trying to get him to stand up. Patrick resisted stubbornly and the man tightened his grip on Patrick's arm and yanked him to his feet.

"I'll take this one," the man said gruffly.

"Very good, Gosact. Your father will be very pleased," the raider replied as he unfastened Patrick from the pole. Gosact counted out some coins and handed them to the raider.

The only good thing about this, Patrick thought, was not being attached to the ale slave anymore.

Patrick now found himself being led by a rope around his neck through a dark forest, the wood of Fochlad, as he would later learn. The man leading him, Gosact, rode a white horse.

"You will work for my father, Chief Miliucc," Gosact said. Gosact seemed to know enough British for Patrick to understand him.

"I'll work for no one!" Patrick said through gritted teeth. Despite all that he had been through, he was still defiant.

"Oh, you'll work for us all right," Gosact countered, pulling hard on the rope. The rope burned Patrick's neck. "I'll beat the work out of you if I have to!"

Patrick tried to study Gosact as he was pulled behind him, keeping a mean eye on him. He had never been beaten before in his life. People had always bowed to him and obeyed him. He had never done any hard work before. He could feel the anger and hatred swelling up inside of him, making him hot with fury.

So many questions bombarded Patrick's mind. He had never felt so much fear, suspicion, and anger all at once.

The two reached Miliucc's fort by dusk. The mist and fading

light made it very hard to see. Patrick was famished and filthy. He hadn't eaten a proper meal in what seemed like days. All he wanted to do was to crawl in a hole and die.

There were a dozen or so small mud huts scattered on either side of a dirt path that wound its way to the fort. The living conditions seemed so primitive compared with his villa back in Britain. The fort, or rath, was laid out in a complete circle, surrounded by a fence of sharp, wooden poles standing on a raised ring of earth.

Gosact led Patrick through a gate in the fence. A slave came and took Gosact's horse from him and led him to a nearby shed. Patrick went to make his way to what looked like the main dwelling house but Gosact pulled him back.

"No!" he grunted and pointed to a rough, wooden hut.

"Even the slaves that lived on my father's villa lived in better conditions than this," thought Patrick.

A man came out of the main house and walked over to Patrick and Gosact. He had dark greying hair and a long, trailing moustache. The man looked like Gosact, only older. He had a hardened look to his face.

The man looked Patrick over, studying him carefully. As he was being inspected, Patrick could see a flesc, a golden bracelet on the man's right arm, the mark of a chief. It had been a long time since Patrick found himself so close to something so fine and beautiful.

"He's got a feisty spirit, this one," Gosact informed his father.

"He'll do. The mountain will soon deal with him. Take him to the slave house," Miliucc grunted.

Free of the rope, Patrick entered what was to be his new home and looked around disdainfully. The room was dark and rustic. There was a rough, low table in the middle of the room. Straw mats were lying on the dirt floor against one of the walls.

Two older men and a youth a little older than Patrick were sitting at the table eating something out of bowls. Patrick kept standing in the doorway, too proud to even acknowledge their gestures. After a few minutes, his starvation won over and Patrick walked over to the men and sat down at the end of one of the benches. He had no idea what was in the bowls, but he felt like he could eat anything. His insides were screaming at him.

One of the men pushed a bowl toward Patrick. "Here," the man said.

Patrick devoured the contents of the bowl so fast he didn't even know what he ate. He looked up to see the two men staring at him.

The man who handed him the food seemed to be able to speak his language. "You must be the new slave whose gonna take care of the sheep," the man said.

"I'm not taking care of any sheep!" Patrick protested defiantly, his vigor coming back to him. "And I'm not a slave!"

The other slaves looked at one another and laughed.

All his energy had left him again and he didn't have the strength to argue back. After all that he had been through this week, Patrick felt like he could sleep for days.

"My name's Aelric" the oldest man said. "This is Berach," Aelric said, pointing to the other man. "This is Bain," Aelric nodded over at the youth who was busy eating. Bain looked up briefly from his bowl and sneered at Patrick.

"I am Patrick, son of Calpurnius, of the town of Bannavem," Patrick said with a yawn. "And when my father finds out what has happened to me, this Miliucc had better watch out."

Aelric and Berach laughed again. Bain stood up straight and glared at Patrick. "You're just a lowly sheep slave. You're nobody now."

Patrick didn't care. He was too tired. He lay down on one of the rough mats next to the wall, turning his back to the men.

"Well, get some sleep now, little Roman, because tomorrow you'll be going to the mountain."

Patrick didn't even hear what Aelric had said. He was already sound asleep. He didn't even feel the fleas crawling over him, biting him as he slept. Tossing and turning in a fitful sleep that night, images of his grandfather's death haunted Patrick's dreams.

Chapter 7

The Beating

Early the next morning Patrick was wakened by Aelric prodding him. "Come on, I have to show you around before you go to the mountain." Patrick downed the mushy porridge that was set on the table before him. Defiantly he stayed put on the bench and glared at Aelric, resisting the urge to scratch his arms and legs.

"I'm not going out to any mountain," Patrick said, glaring at Aelric.

"You had better come with me, boy," Aelric insisted, his voice growing sterner. "You don't want me to have to go and get Master Gosact."

"Go and get him; see if I care!" Patrick scolded.

"Oh, you'll care." Aelric left Patrick on the bench and walked out the door of the hut, shaking his head and sighing as he went.

In a few moments Gosact's huge frame filled the doorway. Patrick felt all the anger rise up inside him again at the sight of the man who had bought him.

Gosact stepped into the hut and with one swift motion grabbed Patrick and forced him to stand up, knocking over the bench. Then he slapped Patrick across the face with his giant hand. Patrick winced from the pain and staggered backwards. Gosact took hold of him again and shoved him out the door.

Tumbling head over heels out on to the damp ground, Patrick was dazed by the sunlight after coming from the dark hut. Gosact dragged Patrick over to a rough wooden post that was driven into the ground. Some shackles were lying on the earth, chained to the post. Gosact locked Patrick's hands and feet into the shackles, and then ripped his cloak from his body. Then Gosact drew out a whip from under the brat draped over his shoulders.

"You WILL work for me!" Gosact roared as he flung the whip against Patrick's bare back. Fighting back tears, Patrick tried to keep his face hard as the pain shot through him like lightning bolts.

"I hate you!" Patrick screamed. The outburst caused Gosact to make the whip smack him even harder.

After ten lashes Gosact lowered his whip and stormed back to the hall. Patrick watched him go with loathing in his tear-filled eyes. He slumped to the ground, his back aching and bleeding. He could still taste blood in his mouth from when Gosact had slapped him. Patrick tried to focus his eyes, but everything around him started to become blurry. His head was swimming and he slowly slipped into unconsciousness.

When he woke up Patrick found himself lying face down on a mat in the slave hut. He could feel a warm sponge being tenderly pressed against his throbbing back. A woman was humming to herself as she soaked his torn flesh. How long he had sat chained to the post after his whipping he did not know.

"You would do well to obey your masters, Patrick," she said. The woman applied some cloth bandages to his back. The sound of her moving around the room was soon followed by Aelric's voice.

"How is he, Cara?" Aelric asked.

"He'll make it. He'll be sore, but he'll be fine," Cara replied tenderly.

"I hope you've learned your lesson," Aelric spoke to Patrick. "When you've finished your porridge, meet me outside."

Cara gently helped Patrick stand up. There was kindness in her eyes. This was the first time anyone had showed any sympathy or care for him since he had been captured.

Coming to his senses quickly by the wet mist stinging his face, Patrick hobbled outside. His whole body ached with each step. Glancing around, Patrick took in his surroundings. The main dwelling house was a large, round structure made of interwoven twigs and branches that seemed to be plastered with mud and clay. Reeds were laid up in a cone shape to a steep point, forming the roof. Some Irish wolf hounds lay by the entrance, keeping watch. Smaller buildings were scattered nearby which were used for storing grain and equipment. He could see a woman taking loaves out of a bread oven. There was what seemed to be a granary, and a husking/winnowing area, as well as a cheese house. A few rough pens housed some animals. Geese and chickens strutted noisily trying to peck at grain that was dropped on the ground. And there was the slave's building which Patrick had just come from, one half for the men and the other for the women. Everything was enclosed by the circular fence.

This place was so different from Bannavem. There was no town here. Just this fort and a few huts outside it.

Patrick shuddered as he walked past the whipping post. His back throbbed with every pulse of his heart. The post stood there as a reminder of what would happen if slaves caused trouble.

Standing ominously just outside the main house was a tall man wearing a dark brown hooded cloak. A jet-black raven was perched on the man's shoulder. The raven let out an ear-piercing screech as Patrick looked over in their direction. Patrick couldn't see the face underneath the heavy hood, but he could feel the man staring at him, sending chills up and down his spine.

Patrick found Aelric just outside the blacksmith hut. When he moved in closer Patrick could see Berach striking a piece of hot iron with a hammer, sending sparks flying everywhere. The older man he had seen talking with Gosact was in the hut looking over some tools.

"That's Master Miliucc," Aelric said to Patrick in a lowered voice. "He's Gosact's father, one of the chiefs of the northern Dalariada tuath, in the kingdom of Ulaid."

"So, he's the man who owns me," thought Patrick. Then he questioned Aelric, "Who's that creepy guy with the raven on his shoulder?"

"That's Odhrain. He's a druid priest. Stay out of his way and do as you're told. He could put a curse on you."

Rolling his eyes, Patrick thought to himself, "I'm not afraid of some silly magic man."

Aelric and Patrick made their way to a back gate in the fence. "What do you do?" Patrick asked Aelric.

"I work with the crops, planting and harvesting," Aelric answered. "Well, it's time for you to work as a slave now, if you're ready to do as you're told."

Outside the gate was an enclosure holding the sheep. "You'll have to take the sheep out to graze, and then make sure they're back in here at dusk," Aelric said. "Wolves can attack the sheep if left out in the dark."

"So, what happened to the slave who herded the sheep before me?" Patrick asked.

"We think he died. He went mad up on the mountain and just disappeared," Aelric remarked. "Too many beatings," he added with a patronizing look on his face.

"Great," thought Patrick as a shiver ran down his spine.

"And don't you try and make a run for it out there!" Aelric warned. "They'll be after you. There's only one thing worse than being a slave, and that's a runaway slave!"

Chapter 8

The Mountain

As Patrick hiked out toward the Braid Valley with the sheep, he caught his first glimpse of Slemish Mountain. Its massive bulk rose up from the earth, haunting the countryside with its eerie presence.

Patrick remembered the path that led from his villa in Britain back to Bannavem. Oh, how he wished he could have Maxi with him now. He remembered looking at the sheep grazing in the fields as he walked into the town. He had watched his father's servants take care of sheep many a day. But he had never stooped so low as to take care of one himself. And now Patrick found himself the lowest of the lowest of slaves. Keeping sheep was considered as low as you could get in Ireland, even lower than herding cattle and keeping pigs. How humiliated Patrick felt. He kept thinking over and over in his mind, he was now a fudir, a captive.

Patrick hugged the thin cloak Cara had given him tight around his scrawny frame. "Would he ever be warm again? Did the sun ever shine in this place?" he wondered as the Light drizzle wet his skin.

The path he trod was lined with a blackthorn hedge. The mountain, or "sliabh" as the locals called it, loomed in front of him.

Patrick pulled a stick out of the hedge, leaning on it as he walked to ease the pain in his body. He hoped he would only have to use it for walking.

Patrick managed to find the sheep fold Aelric had told him about, right at the base of the mountain. A small shelter made from rocks and mud was all there was, connected to a circular wall of rocks that was the sheep pen. There was no gate, only an opening in the wall. Patrick entered the sheep fold, trying not to step on the dung scattered about the turfy ground. Inside the shelter there was no bed, no table, no chair. Nothing.

Sitting down on the damp ground and leaning his shoulder against the cold stone wall of the shelter, Patrick began to weep. He couldn't take it anymore. All the pent- up frustration, fear, anxiety, and anger came pouring out of him. For what seemed like hours he sobbed uncontrollably, crying bitter tears.

There, inside the foul smelling, cold and barren sheep shelter Patrick wrestled with his thoughts. He wrestled with God. He was completely undone. He was nobody now. He was cold, hungry, weak, and helpless. No one back in Britain would recognize the dirty boy now dressed in tattered rags. He had no family here, no father and grandfather. He was no longer the son of Calpurnius. He was no longer Roman. He was a slave, a fudir. He was completely and totally undone. He was nothing.

"God, what do you want with me?" he cried. "If you are real, reveal yourself to me! Why is this happening? Why am I here? Why did my grandfather have to die? Will I ever see my family again? I don't deserve this! I hate you! Why can't I just die?"

The sound of footsteps woke him. Lifting his face off the dirty floor, Patrick grabbed his blackthorn stick. He peered out quietly to see Aelric entering the fold.

"Well, looks like our noble Roman boy has had himself a good old cry!" laughed Aelric. "It's nearly dusk, and you had better get those sheep back before Gosact comes looking for them!"

Patrick had forgotten all about the sheep. A feeling of sheer panic went racing through his body. He ran out of the sheep fold and couldn't believe his eyes. The sheep were gone! He turned desperately toward Aelric. "What am I going to do?"

"I told you to get those sheep in before dark. If I were you, I'd get yourself back to the rath. Beg his forgiveness and mercy, and pray to Cernunnos that his sheep are found," Aelric said.

Patrick could feel a big lump in his gut. His heart beat faster and faster as he and Aelric neared the rath. "What's going to happen to me now?" Patrick thought. Images of Gosact beating him came surging back to his mind. His back ached with each running step, reminding him of what was going to happen again.

"Well, a shepherd doesn't need two hands," Aelric pretended to console Patrick. "Just hope Gosact doesn't decide to cut off both your hands!"

As they left the hawthorn hedge and caught sight of the sheep pen, Aelric started to chuckle. There in the pen were the sheep, huddled in a tight bundle and bleating at the approach of the two slaves. Aelric was bellowing with laughter now.

Patrick, his pride hurt and his anger raging, kicked the gate of the pen and then walked into the rath in a huff.

Chapter 9

Worship in the Woods

The next morning found Patrick out in the sheep fold near the base of Slemish again. He was glad to be rid of Aelric and Berach and their constant ridicule and jokes. The sheep were grazing contentedly in the fields below the mountain.

Patrick felt utterly miserable. Looking around him he thought of trying to escape. "If they do catch me," he thought, "the worst that could happen to me is they could kill me, and that would be better than being stuck here taking care of dirty, old sheep." Grabbing his stick, he headed toward the wood. The tiny, white snowdrop flowers were just poking their heads above the dewy grass. A babbling stream trickled its way out of the wood and wound its way through Miliucc's fields.

Patrick stopped for a moment, listening with his ears perked. He thought he could hear singing. The singing got clearer as Patrick neared the forest. It was coming from the edge of the wood. Patrick couldn't believe his ears! They were singing in Latin! And he knew the song! Whoever they were, they were singing the Twenty Third Psalm!

Sudden memories of the church in Bannavem and his grandfather came rushing into his mind. Memories he had been trying so hard to forget hit him like a lightning bolt. Despite the aching in his back, Patrick found himself running as fast as he could towards the singing. Music he had once tried to get away from was now drawing him eagerly toward it.

Patrick reached the edge of the wood and walked a short distance to a small clearing. About half a dozen people sat on fallen logs they had turned into seats. Cara, the woman who had cleaned his wounds after his whipping, was there. He also recognized one of the older women. She was one of his father's servants! Eda was her name. She must have been captured that same night Patrick and Lupita had been taken. Lupita! She might know something about Lupita!

Patrick remained hidden where he was behind a Rowan tree, his eyes fixed on the gathering. Along with the two women, there was another younger woman and two other men. One of the men started to speak. He spoke British! After saying a prayer, the man started to quote from the Bible. This must be a Sunday worship service, Patrick thought. He had lost all sense of time and days since being captured.

Patrick listened as the man quoted from Psalm 40: "I waited patiently for the LORD; he inclined to me and heard my cry. He drew me up from the pit of destruction, out of the miry bog, and set my feet upon a rock, making my steps secure. He put a new song in my mouth, a song of praise to our God. Many will see and fear and put their trust in the LORD.... As for you, O LORD, you will not restrain your mercy from me; your steadfast love and your faithfulness will ever preserve me!... Be pleased, O LORD, to deliver me! O LORD, make haste to help me!"

The words cut through Patrick's heart. He listened eagerly to what the man had to say about the scripture. It felt so good to hear someone speak his native language. But the experience reminded him so much of his grandfather. He couldn't help feeling the hurt and anguish creep back into his heart again.

This was the first time he had ever really listened to a sermon before. Back in Bannavem he never paid any attention to what the priests said. They never had anything interesting to say. But this time he found the words so comforting. He felt a peace rush over him as he listened.

Now was his chance to speak to his father's woman servant. Patrick stepped out from his hiding place and walked slowly to where the group was now standing, talking among themselves.

Cara saw Patrick first and seemed happy to see him. "How are you feeling?" she asked with her eyes full of concern.

"I've been better," Patrick fumbled for words. He felt ashamed at not having anything nice to say to her. He had never been kind to slaves before. He wasn't particularly mean to them, only when they deserved it. But he usually never bothered about them. If they did their work and didn't cause him trouble, he left them alone. Cara didn't seem to mind, though. Her eyes still poured out warmth and compassion in a way that Patrick felt drawn to her. She reminded him of his grandfather.

"Patrick!" Eda hollered out as she came hobbling over at the sight of Patrick. Patrick shirked away at his father's servant being so familiar with him. Then he remembered he was now a slave as well. Now he was equal with the slaves that worked his father's fields and worked in his father's house.

"Eda, do you know where Lupita is?" Patrick questioned, the anxiety rising in his heart. "Is she okay?"

Eda looked down and backed away slightly, remembering who she was and who he once was. "We got separated, Patrick," Eda said, tears forming in her eyes. "It was so terrible. I lost sight of her. Lupita was put into a different boat. I'm sorry Patrick."

Chapter 10

Bain and Odhrain

Patrick quietly started on his way back to the sheepfold with so much confusion in his head. He felt disheartened and alone but at the same time he felt he had been given a tiny ray of hope. He still believed with all his heart that Lupita was alive. She had to be.

Patrick also couldn't get the words of the sermon out of his head. "I wonder if they meet every Sunday," Patrick thought. In his excitement at hearing the singing, seeing Eda, and then the possibility he might hear of Lupita, he had forgotten to ask Eda about the gathering and the service. And he had forgotten all about trying to escape. How could he escape with Lupita still here somewhere anyway?

Patrick continued his way across the field. He wasn't even aware of the cattle grazing nearby. Suddenly he was brought abruptly out of his day-dreaming by a stone hitting his back, sending a sharp pain soaring through his body.

Turning around, Patrick caught sight of Bain with another stone clenched in his fist, about to hurtle it toward him. He ducked just in time as it skimmed the top of his head and landed with a thud on the ground.

"Get yourself and these filthy sheep out of here!" Bain roared.

Patrick picked up the stone that had hit him. With anger rising, he threw his arm back and hurled the stone in Bain's direction. Bain stepped to the side and the stone thudded to a stop against the side of a calf. The startled calf let out a bleat and skipped toward its mother.

"Oh, you're gonna get it now!" Bain cried. "Wait till Master Miliucc hears about this. It'll be another beating for you!"

All that happened to him this time was a firm scolding. Gosact happened to be away so Bain reported the incident to Chief Miliucc who reprimanded Patrick. Miliucc was firm on obedience but seemed not to be prone to violence like Gosact.

As Patrick stepped out the front door of the main house a bony hand reached out and grabbed his arm. A raven screeched and flew off to a nearby tree.

"You are trouble, young Briton," the druid whispered in a raspy voice. His grip tightened, squeezing Patrick's arm.

Patrick froze, that familiar chill running down his spine. Odhrain's hand was like ice, the coolness penetrating throughout Patrick's body. The whole world seemed to go dark as Odhrain's jet black eyes penetrated deep into his soul. After what seemed like an eternity Odhrain finally let Patrick go. Without looking back, Patrick ran to the slave hut as fast as he could to get away from that creepy druid.

Back in the slave hut, Patrick collapsed on his mat and tried to shake off the horrible incident. He tried to bring back the words spoken at the service that had given him such peace. Would God deliver him out of this miry pit he found himself in? Could he trust in a God who allowed him to be dumped into this awful place? Patrick tossed and turned that night, a fitful sleep wrestling with him. In his dreams he saw the stone hurling through the air directly at him. Then he saw himself as a lifeless, useless stone stuck in a muddy bog. He was unable to move, covered all over in filth. And then he felt someone mighty and strong take hold of him and lift him out of the mud and set him securely on top of a rock wall.

Chapter 11

Market

It was now March and three months had passed since he had been captured. Patrick spent most of his time out in the sheep pen by the mountain. His life was now consumed with sheep. Up at the crack of dawn, he had to stay outside during the cold, rain, and snow. Every night found Patrick trying to stay awake watching for lambs. Sometimes he would bring the new-born lambs into the pen and sleep in the entrance to keep them safe. He had never had any time at all for the animals on his father's villa. He was now doing tasks that he would have considered beneath him, dirty jobs only for a slave. He still had to keep reminding himself that he was a slave.

Life was extremely hard. Patrick spent a lot of time alone. Gosact always had some reason to beat him. Bain was always instigating trouble. And that foul Odhrain was always watching him like a black shadow.

The long hours spent on his own gave him many opportunities to think about his life. God had always seemed so very far away to Patrick and now he seemed as far away as ever. Patrick began to feel as if God was punishing him. This was the only explanation he could think of for why he was captured and taken to this forsaken land to be a slave.

"I hate it here!" Patrick screamed as loud as he could as he made the daily rounds of the fields, making sure the sheep were all accounted for. "I hate the Irish, and I hate sheep!"

Walking along the stream that meandered through the field where Miliucc's sheep were grazing, Patrick decided to hike to the very top of Slemish. Using his blackthorn staff to help balance himself, he gingerly waded through the gushing water. He was careful not to get swept away by the racing stream full of melting winter snow. Sitting on a rock to rub his numb feet, Patrick watched the scrawny lambs jump and frolic, skipping around their mothers. The heather plants were starting to show off their purple color. Spring was in the air, but Patrick could still feel the chill of the wind that came in off the sea.

Stepping onto rocky ledges and grabbing for bits of grassy tufts, Patrick made his way slowly up the mountain. Half-way up he stopped and perched himself on a flattened outcropping of rock. He could see the little sheep fold and the meandering stream. The sheep looked like tiny white specks. Patrick watched the activity of the little people working in and around the rath.

When he reached the summit, he felt like the wind was going to blow his head off. His braccae and cloak flapped against him violently. The top of Mount Slemish was mostly flat and it felt good to walk on level ground again. Patrick stood and looked around him in all directions. The Braid Valley stretched out before him to the north and west. To the south and east he could see the dense Wood of Fochlad. And past the fields and woods, somewhere in the distance, was the sea. It had been a long time since Patrick had seen the sea. He squinted and tried as hard as he could to find the sea. He knew it was there, out beyond the horizon. And beyond the sea was Britain.

Patrick knelt on the ground, the tears flooding his eyes at the memory of his family. "One day, I will get back," he resolved.

"Here comes our little Roman," Aelric said to Berach as Patrick stepped into the hut. Glaring at the two men, Patrick sat down on the bench and took his share of meat and bread from the bowls on the table. He was famished after the hike up the mountain. And he was in no mood for Aelric's insults and antics.

"And what did our little Roman do today?" Aelric taunted.

"Patrick!" a voice bellowed. Aelric and Berach went silent.

Patrick whirled his head around to see Gosact standing in the doorway.

"Yes, Master."

"Tomorrow we will take some of the lambs to the market. Be ready at sunrise."

"Yes, Master." At least the appearance of Gosact had silenced the two men.

Patrick watched Gosact pick out the choicest of his lambs. He tied the lambs together using a long rope.

"These lambs had better bring a good price," Gosact spoke sternly to Patrick. "There will be a beating waiting for you when we get back if they don't sell well!"

Gosact hoisted himself onto his white horse and motioned for Patrick to follow him. Following Gosact around the edge of the rath, they came to the dirt path he had been led along the first day he had been bought. He pulled the sheep along the path, past the huts where the tribe's people lived. A little girl with long, dark hair and pretty, blue eyes waved at Patrick.

Gosact led his horse into the wood. They went a short distance till they came to a clearing. A ring of tall, ancient oak trees stood in the middle. Gosact and Patrick walked to the trees and Odhrain slithered out from behind one of them. His raven let out a blood curdling cry as Gosact took the line of lambs from Patrick. Odhrain laid his hands on the lambs one by one and chanted some spells or prayers over them. Then he turned to Patrick and Patrick felt his body stiffen as if turning to stone.

"You had better pray to Cernunnos," the druid croaked, waving a bony finger at him. "Things will not go well for you if you don't!"

The two travellers left the clearing and didn't speak a word to one another. Patrick was glad to be out of the wood. He hated to admit it, but he was afraid of Odhrain. And he hated the very sight of Gosact. He comforted himself with the thought that he might see Lupita. Maybe she would be at the market or maybe he would hear something of her! That thought gave him a little hope.

The market was a bustling place. Slaves were driving stubborn sheep, cattle, and pigs into waiting pens, prodding them with their staffs. Chiefs and nobles were inspecting livestock and calling out prices. There was a druid sitting at a table writing dots and lines on a piece of leather. Patrick guessed it was some way of recording livestock and the prices they sold for. There were men selling bread, ale, cheese, and fish from makeshift stalls. The concoction of smells wafted toward Patrick's nose, making his stomach turn itself inside out with hunger. He hadn't tasted good food in so long.

Trying not to focus on the gymnastics his ravenous stomach was performing, Patrick watched the throngs of people involved in the commotion of buying, selling, and bartering. As he and Gosact passed by where the newly captured slaves were being sold, Patrick kept his eyes out for Lupita. Maybe she would be here on some errand for her master. Or maybe she would be sold again.

Gosact directed Patrick to which pen to herd the lambs into. The lambs bleated nervously as if they knew something was going to happen to them. Patrick fetched some water for them with a calf skin bucket.

Men bartered with Gosact all afternoon. There were no signs of Lupita. The other slaves Patrick had talked to had never heard of her. Feeling hopeless, he sat in the dirt in front of the pen and devoured the cheese and bread Gosact had thrown at him grudgingly.

Soon, just one lamb was left. All day men looked at the lamb and just walked on. Gosact argued to the best of his ability, trying hard to sell his last lamb. The lone lamb stood in the pen bleating, staring at Patrick. Feeling overwhelming pity and empathy, Patrick began to despair, strangely not for himself, but for the lamb. No one wanted him or cared for him. The lamb was all alone, at the mercy of others.

A rough box on the left ear jolted Patrick out of his thoughts. "You're going to get more than that when we get back to the rath!" Gosact roared. "Come on, you lazy slave. Get that worthless lamb and let's go."

Patrick grabbed the rope, made a loop and slipped it gently over the lamb's head. He kneeled on the ground and rubbed its head behind the ears. For the first time in a long while Patrick began to care for something.

Back at the rath, Patrick sat chained to the post again. Gosact had kicked him and had hit him hard across the face. He could feel a welt forming on his right cheek. Gosact had ranted at him the whole way back from the market about how it was his fault the lamb did not sell. Night was falling and Patrick shivered in the cold.

His anger gave way to despair. "Oh, God, what are you doing to me? Why is all this happening?"

His grandfather would tell him to trust in God. His grandfather would tell him that God loves him. How could God love him if he was allowing all this to happen? How could he ever put his trust in God now?

When Patrick woke the next morning, he stared in disbelief and shock at the lifeless lamb. The lamb that had not been sold was now dead. Even this tiny little lamb, that Patrick had felt some connection to, felt some pity for, had been taken away from him. Just when he had made a friend, just when he was able to feel close to something again, it was just stripped away from him.

Numbly, Patrick stared at the other sheep grazing. He watched their fat, woolly bodies slowly meandering about the field, pulling up grass. He hated them. He vowed to never feel love for anything or anyone ever again.

Chapter 12

Bealtaine

It had been a few weeks since Patrick had been able to meet with the little group of slaves in the wood. Because they were slaves, they weren't always able to meet every Sunday. He never knew who would be there or who was able to make it.

One certain Sunday Patrick made sure the sheep were grazing in the field closest to the wood. He walked with anticipation, his walking staff thumping the ground with every step. Patrick looked forward to the meetings in the wood. They were a little bit of a connection with Britain. He now sat among the little group instead of hiding behind the Rowan tree. Patrick hung on every word that Killian spoke. Somehow the words made the anger he felt dissipate a little. Something seemed to stir his soul when he met with the others for worship.

A stone hit him in the shoulder. "Here we go again," Patrick sighed to himself. Patrick knew who had thrown it without turning around.

"Get lost, Bain. Leave me alone."

"So, you're one of those silly Christians!" Bain snickered at Patrick.

"What's it to you?" Patrick replied, annoyed.

"You actually believe in that silly God who died! No wonder you're such a pig brain," Bain taunted. "Lugh is more powerful than your God."

"The only reason you believe in Lugh is because you're afraid of Odhrain!" shouted Patrick.

"I'll tell Odhrain that you don't believe in Lugh!" said Bain, running back toward the rath.

"Hey, leave him alone!" shouted Killian at Bain. The other slaves turned when they heard the shouting.

"Oh, don't worry about him," Patrick said while rolling his eyes.

As he sat among the other worshipping slaves he couldn't help thinking about the confrontation with Bain. He still wasn't sure there was only one true God. The people sitting with him were confident in their belief in God. His grandfather was genuine. But his father had no time for God. His father paid lip service to God but that was it. The Romans had their gods. And here among the Irish he was being exposed to a whole new variety of gods to believe in.

After the service Killian approached Patrick with a concerned look on his face.

"Patrick, you do not realize how much God loves you," Killian spoke softly. The two sat on one of the log benches in the clearing.

"If God does love me, then why is all this happening?" questioned Patrick, his voice full of anguish.

"God disciplines those he loves. He is drawing you to himself. He is stripping you of everything precious to you because he wants his Son to be most precious to you."

"Then it's all my fault!" Patrick wailed in exasperation. "It's my fault my grandfather died. It's my fault that I was captured. It's my fault that I'm stuck here taking care of sheep in this awful place. God is punishing me!"

"God is drawing you to himself," Killian calmly answered. "God has to bring you to a low place, strip you of everything, so that all you can see and want is Christ! He is making you realize that you are nothing so He can become everything! And God is doing this because of his love for you!"

Killian spoke with such tenderness and passion. He really meant what he said. But Patrick still wasn't sure. He just wasn't ready to trust yet.

"But I am someone!" Patrick wailed. "I am a Roman nobleman's son. I don't belong here! I don't want to be stripped of everything! I am no slave! No one is my master!"

The morning sun felt warm on Patrick's face as he walked the well-worn path from the sheep fold to Miliucc's rath. It was May and the Irish were celebrating the feast of Bealtaine in honor of the god Bel. Bealtaine marked the beginning of summer when the cattle were driven out of their barns and into the summer pastures. This was a very important holiday to the cattle breeding Irish. The tuath was celebrating the holiday at Miliucc's rath this year.

The rath was abuzz with all the preparations. Yellow flowers adorned all the doors, gates, windows, and byres. Even the cattle were wearing garlands of yellow flowers around their necks.

Inside, the fort was bustling with activity. Eda was grinding wheat into meal with a quern. She would then use the meal to make bread. Patrick watched as Cara cooked large pieces of meat for the feast. The water hissed and spat as the hot stones were lowered into the large wood-lined hole filled with water.

Patrick stepped into the slave hut to get his breakfast. The sight of Aelric made him burst out laughing. Aelric's clothing was turned completely inside out. He was wearing his braccae and shirt inside out, and his cloak as well.

"Aelric, why on earth are you wearing your clothes like that?" Patrick questioned, still laughing.

"You shouldn't laugh, Patrick," Aelric said. "I don't want to offend the si. They are especially active this day."

Seeing a grown man wearing his clothes inside out to ward off little fairies was just too much for Patrick. He just about got his porridge down without choking.

Patrick, Aelric, and Berach joined the rest of the tuath outside the rath. All members of the tuath, even the slaves, were ordered to gather at the east side to begin the border ritual. Odhrain started the procession with Miliucc and Gosact following. Everyone else in the tuath walked behind them. The chiefs carried seeds of grain, farming tools, the first well water drawn that morning, and an herb called vervain. The procession began at the east side of the fort and paraded to the south, west, and then the north sides, mimicking a sunward direction. At each side a ritual was performed to ward off the si and to protect the farm produce and encourage fertility of the livestock, especially the cattle.

The procession then marched out to where two enormous bonfires were blazing. Odhrain and some other druids huddled together and started chanting. Patrick watched a youth who had been chosen, take a torch and light it from one of the bonfires. The youth then ran back to the rath to re-light the household fire, which had been doused.

Miliucc handed one of the druids the end of a rope that was hung around the neck of a cow. The druid raised a long knife and slit the cow's throat, its blood spilling to the ground. Another druid caught some of the blood in a bowl, then handed the bowl to Miliucc. Miliucc raised the bowl in the air and then brought it to his lips and sipped it. Miliucc handed the bowl to Gosact who did the same. Then the druid poured the rest of the blood onto the earth, chanting prayers for the herd's health and safety.

Patrick watched all the rituals with fascination. Feeling confused, he thought of the tiny group of Christians that worshiped in the wood. He just didn't know what to believe.

With the rest of the tuath, Patrick watched as Bain drove the cattle herd between the two huge bonfires while the druid priests continued their monotonous chanting. The cattle became lost in the thick, swirling smoke as they were driven through. The smoke purified the cattle and protected them against evil spirits. He couldn't help but remember the Christmas day when he and Flavius had taken part in the Sol Invictus celebration. "I wonder where Flavius is and what he's doing now?" wondered Patrick.

The rituals over, all the men of the tuath gathered inside the main hall to start their feasting. Miliucc and Gosact sat regally at the head table with the other chiefs, devouring the choicest joints of meat. Slaves were kept busy scurrying around tables, pouring out plenty of mead to the greedy warriors. Huge black cauldrons of iron were simmering on the hearth, spitting out steam. On top the tables sat various earthen vessels richly decorated, to hold food and drink.

Patrick had to stand at attention along the wall in case one of the chiefs required some duty of him. He tried to remain in the shadows so he would not be called upon. The noise in the room was deafening as the men were becoming drunk with the mead. Each warrior yelled louder to outdo his companion in telling his boastful tale of his victories in war.

Two warriors started fighting over a flagon of mead. One claimed he had the right to it because he was the warrior with the greatest distinction in battle. "I've slain more men than you have," he roared, lunging forward, shoving the other warrior to the ground. Soon all the men were throwing punches. One of the other slaves ducked just in time as a dagger that was thrown sunk into the wooden wall behind him. Patrick cowered in a corner, his eyes gaping at the scene. Other punches were being thrown now and very soon a brawl developed among the warriors.

"Now is my chance to get out of here", Patrick thought. "They won't even notice I'm gone in all this mayhem."

Just as he was trying to make a run for it, the dark, shadowy figure of Odhrain crept out of a dark corner and blocked the doorway.

"Don't worship the Christian God," Odhrain warned, focusing his steel eyes on Patrick. "If you do, there will be trouble!"

Chapter 13

True Freedom!

Patrick found himself spending more and more time alone. He began to enjoy the solitude of the mountain, often climbing up to the summit on a clear day and pretending he could see Britain on the horizon. He would imagine he was still at home with Maxi and think of his grandfather. He felt free on the mountain. Strangely, the mountain had become his home.

With just his thoughts for company, Patrick became very aware of his unbelief and insignificance. Like a hammer striking an anvil, he felt every sin hit him hard. No matter how hard he tried to resurrect his pride and importance, he felt so small.

Patrick's life was all about sheep now, lambing them in the spring, shearing their fleeces in summer, slaughtering them for meat in the autumn, and constantly watching over them.

Bain and Odhrain were always lurking around, constantly watching him. For some reason, Odhrain especially hated Patrick. He heard the gossip and the rumors from the other slaves. Something about an old prophecy. "Some trick of Odhrain's to stir up hatred and suspicion," thought Patrick.

The July sun was shining its rays down warmly upon Slemish Mountain. At least it was bearable to be outside now, although it still rained a lot. "I will get back to Britain someday," Patrick sighed. He worked his way down the mountain side, stepping on the familiar stones and tufts of grass that stuck out between the juts of rock. The purple heather was vibrant in the sun.

Patrick tried taking his grandfather's and Killian's advice. He tried trusting in God, but found it so hard, especially when it seemed like every time he did start to trust, something bad happened. He would be dashed to pieces like a piece of pottery hitting a hard rock. When Patrick tried praying, he felt like he was just stammering to a rock wall.

There were so many questions bombarding Patrick's mind. He wished so much that he could talk with his grandfather. His grandfather would make everything right. He always did. Patrick felt so alone, so empty, and he was utterly exhausted. He found he didn't even have the energy to be angry anymore. Patrick didn't realize it, but his life was being stripped from him. He was becoming nothing.

This had been a tough week for Patrick. Some of the young lambs had been taken and killed by wolves. Of course, Gosact blamed Patrick and had beaten him severely for it. With each smack of the whip against his back, another layer of pride was stripped away from him. Patrick felt that he could not be brought any lower. Everything he tried to hold on to was being taken away.

Sitting with Killian in the clearing, Patrick began to pour his heart out. "I feel like a complete failure," he sighed. "I have ruined everything. Everything is my fault. I turned away from God and so now he is punishing me. My grandfather died. My sister was taken. God had me captured and brought here, and now God wants me to be a slave here in this miserable place to suffer for my sins. God has turned his back on me. I have nothing left."

"Patrick, God has taken away everything so that Christ can become everything to you! Your problem is you still dwell too much on yourself. God isn't punishing you. He is getting you to realize you need Christ. God has caused all these things to happen to you because he is drawing you to himself. Yes, you are nothing! You need to see that by becoming nothing, Christ becomes your all! Patrick, there is nothing you can do to trust Christ. You cannot change your heart and you certainly cannot escape life. Just let Christ take over your life. You must trust Jesus and let Christ become your Master."

"But I don't want a master!" Patrick replied. "I just want to be free."

"Only Christ gives true freedom," commented Killian. "Only Christ can take away all your guilt and free you of your anger and mistrust. All you must do is trust him. Just cling to Christ."

Patrick thought about the way his grandfather had lived. His grandfather was honest and loving and even treated his servants with respect. And Killian, Cara, and Eda were full of compassion, even toward the people who were so cruel to them. And yet they had a peace and a confidence that Patrick coveted with all his heart. He wondered how they could love life so much and love people the way they did.

Walking back to the rath, Patrick caught a glimpse of Gosact riding away on his white stallion. Anger and bitterness still welled up inside him whenever he saw him. He hated Gosact with an overwhelming intensity. He actually hated all the Irish.

Patrick could feel the weight of his sin like a heavy burden on his back. It was so heavy sometimes he found it hard to breathe. It was like his sin was smacking him in the face and punching him in the stomach. No matter what he did he felt so rotten and dirty. His heart was so black and hard. He realized more than ever how much of a sinner he was, a sinner deserving to go to hell. And this made him very much afraid.

The soft rain dripped off the tree leaves and onto the ground as Patrick sat waiting for Killian to start the service. He kicked at a stone, sending sparks of mud flying into the air. He literally was like a stone stuck in a mud puddle. "Would God really come along and reach down and pull me out?" he thought. "Can I trust God? Can God's power reach even to me?"

With such a heavy heart, Patrick couldn't bring himself to sing along with the others. Lost in his thoughts, he remembered the Scriptures he had learned with his grandfather. He painfully recalled how he used to hate it when his grandfather would make him learn verses from the word of God.

Overcome with guilt, Patrick listened as Killian started to quote the Scriptures. "Today's passage is from the book of Ephesians," Killian began. "But God, being rich in mercy, because of the great love with which he loved us, even when we were dead in our trespasses, made us alive together with Christ – by grace you have been saved."

Suddenly, Patrick felt cut to the heart. It was like the Holy Spirit shot an arrow right through his soul. He continued listening intently to Killian.

"For by grace you have been saved through faith. And this is not of yourselves, lest any man should boast."

He remembered Hebrews 12:2, "The word of God is sharper than a two-edged sword, piercing to the division of soul and spirit . . ." Everything seemed as bright and clear as crystal. As Patrick sat on the wooden log, tears streaming down his face, he believed the truth. And the truth set him free.

Sensing what was going on, Killian had stopped speaking and went to sit next to Patrick, putting his arm around his shoulders. The other worshipers started to pray quietly for Patrick.

"God is calling you, Patrick," Killian said softly.

"I can't go on like this anymore," Patrick sobbed.

With tears streaming down his face, Patrick cried out to his Heavenly Father. He had had enough. "Oh God, have mercy on my soul. I am a sinner. I am sorry for my sin. I need your grace."

As Patrick poured his heart out to the Lord, he felt a warmth spreading through his soul like a flame. He felt the burden of all his guilt and shame lifted. He was truly free!

Killian, Eda, Clara, and the others couldn't hold back tears as they embraced him and welcomed him into the family of God.

Leaving the service, Patrick was compelled to go to the mountain. He was truly free! "I am free!" he yelled at the top of his lungs. "I love you, Lord, my Master! My Lord and my God!"

He wished so much that he could tell his grandfather. His grandfather would be so proud. Potitus had prayed so much for Patrick and had so desired to see this day.

Overjoyed at his newfound freedom and salvation, Patrick felt invincible as he climbed up the mountain. He couldn't wait to share with others how Christ had saved him from sin. He had never felt so much love and joy in his heart before.

In the days to come Patrick would understand how God's Spirit had convicted him of his sin, given him a wonderful knowledge of Jesus Christ as the only Savior, and enabled him to love and embrace the gospel of Jesus Christ.

Chapter 14

God's Healing Power

ven with his new faith in Christ, Patrick continued to feel deep anguish and shame over his sinfulness. At the same time, he felt such a wonder and joy in his Savior and the gospel of God's grace. God the Father chose him to be saved! He found it so amazing that God had compassion on him and loved him, even when he was such a rotten sinner. God's saving power had taken its grip on him and totally transformed him. Patrick realized he had to become a slave so that he could become free in Christ.

Patrick knew now that true freedom wasn't found in living the life of a nobleman. True freedom was found in Christ alone, trusting in Christ for the forgiveness of sins. He still marvelled that he could be so free and still be a dirty slave.

Slowly, Patrick's life was changing. Not just from a Roman decurion's son to a slave but from a selfish, proud, careless youth into a selfless, humble, sensitive, and caring young man.

It was now late autumn, and when the wind came out of the north and east it was cold, and snow could be seen swirling in the air. Patrick had just come down off the mountain where he had spent all morning in prayer. He looked at the sheep grazing, their woolly fleeces keeping them warm. He had grown fond of the sheep and enjoyed taking care of them. The lambs reminded him of being born again in Christ. Watching them run and frolic made him remember how he felt the day God had lifted his burden of sin. He had felt so light and free.

"How's our holy boy today?" Aelric mocked Patrick. "You must be mad, spending all morning on that mountain in the cold!"

"I don't even feel the cold," Patrick replied. "Even on frosty nights the Holy Spirit keeps me warm!"

Aelric just rolled his eyes. The two of them walked along the edge of Fochlod Wood, heading toward the rath.

"Praying to God my Father keeps me from getting lonely," Patrick went on. "And I feel no hunger. I hunger after God. God and his word are food for my soul, nourishment for my being, the sustenance for my very life. I depend upon him."

"You're completely topsy-turvy, Patrick," laughed Aelric. "All this praying and fasting you do. I think you've lost your mind!"

"For me it is throwing myself completely upon the mercy of

Christ. More and more I must become nothing so I can only depend upon him. I need to totally cling to Christ to survive."

"Doesn't your God want sacrifices?" Aelric asked.

"He only requires that we trust him. It's as simple as that!" Patrick explained.

"Doesn't your God ever get angry with you?"

"The Lord is longsuffering, caring and compassionate and full of grace," Patrick expressed with conviction. "And I can pray to God anywhere." He went on. "In the woods, on the mountain, on my mat in the slave hut. And I can pray anytime, during the night, at dawn, during the day, watching the sheep, and even while Gosact is beating me."

Aelric just listened as the two slaves walked in through the gate. But then the old man turned to Patrick with a grim face and said, "Just be careful, Patrick. Watch out for Odhrain. What they are all saying about this prophecy..." Aelric's voice trailed off in a gruff whisper.

"Don't worry, God will take care of me," Patrick assured his friend. Since his conversion, Patrick had grown very fond of Aelric. And even despite Aelric's teasing and taunting, Patrick knew that Aeric had grown to care for him in his own way. Aelric was very curious about this change in Patrick, and Patrick was praying hard for Aelric, hopeful that God would save him, too.

"What's all the commotion?" Patrick asked as he and Aelric entered the slave hut.

"Berach's been hurt badly!" Bain stammered.

Patrick pushed through the crowd and found Berach lying on his mat, blood gushing from a gash in his leg. Clara was hunched over Berach pressing cloths onto the wound, doing all she could to get the bleeding stopped.

"His hammer slipped," Bain spoke rapidly. "Got him in his leg. I heard his cry and brought him in here."

"Is it serious?" Patrick asked.

"It doesn't look good. There's no hope," said Bain. "Odhrain did all he could." Bain gave a disdainful look at Patrick, telling him with his eyes that there was nothing Patrick could do.

Patrick looked at Berach screaming out as he writhed with pain. "We must pray to Almighty God," said Patrick. "God can heal Berach if He wants to."

Patrick knelt on the ground beside Berach. "I'm going to elevate your leg, Berach," he spoke quietly and calmly to the groaning man. Laying his hands on the man's leg while Clara kept the wound covered with the cloth, Patrick began praying. "Oh, Father, please have mercy on Berach. I ask that you please heal his leg. I know you can do all things. I trust him into your care. Show your power and glory through him, in your Son's precious name, Amen."

As Patrick finished his prayer a calmness came over Berach. Patrick started to stand up and Berach gripped his arm. "Thank you, Patrick," he said with a gasping voice.

Patrick smiled down at the wounded man. He was surprised at the love and concern he felt for him, this pagan Irish man who insulted him and taunted him all the time.

The slaves in the hut looked in astonishment at Berach lying calm and at peace. Aelric turned to Clara with a look of amazement. "I can't believe what I just saw!" he exclaimed. "Did that little Roman boy actually do something nice?"

"There's no such god as this 'Father God'," Bain sneered as he stormed out of the hut. Patrick knew Bain didn't approve of what he did. But he didn't care. How could he conceal his love for Christ, and how could he not minister to others this love that God had so graciously shown to him?

More than ever, Patrick felt everyone's eyes upon him. They watched everything he did. Everyone was curious about the change in this slave boy's life. Some were just curious, but some didn't like it. No one was more suspicious than Odhrain.

Odhrain grabbed hold of Patrick one day and shook him violently. "You will not pray to that Father God! I will break you and curse you if you do!"

"You can only do to me what God Almighty allows you to do to me, Odhrain!" Patrick countered. "He may allow you to destroy my body, but you will never be able to destroy my soul!"

Odhrain let Patrick go, shocked by the new confidence of the young slave boy. How dare he talk to him, a druid priest, like that! Odhrain had confided in Miliucc that Patrick was trouble. He had shared with Miliucc about the prophecy, how one from another land would come and overthrow the power of the druids. But Miliucc refused to take his counsel. The truth was that ever since this change had come over Patrick, Miliucc's crops and cattle had begun to prosper greatly and Miliucc attributed this luck to Patrick. Odhrain watched Patrick walk out to the fields with disgust and hatred. He would not let this slave boy take away his power.

Chapter 15

The Power of Prayer

"**W**hat! Are you not going to fight me, you filthy slave?" A drunken Gosact roared at Patrick and punched him in the gut. Patrick doubled over, stiffened with pain.

"Father, please forgive him. He doesn't know what he is doing," Patrick prayed.

"Come on, defend yourself, holy boy!" Gosact smacked Patrick across the face. "I told you not to pray to that God of yours!" Gosact yelled with anger. "And don't let me catch you defying Odhrain again! My father doesn't believe Odhrain's prophecy, but I do! You are nothing but bad luck and trouble. And if I catch you meeting with that group in the clearing, there will be trouble!"

Gosact spat at Patrick, leaving him bent over, holding his stomach.

"Oh Lord, give me strength," Patrick prayed to himself. He picked himself up and limped into the slave hut. Glad that the others were away busy with their tasks, Patrick lay on his mat and cried to God.

"Father God, please forgive me my sins. I'm sorry for the way

I treated those you had placed under my father's care. Please reveal your love to Gosact. Help me to show Christ's love to him. Help me to see these people as you see them. Help me to see them as precious souls in need of your grace. Help me to be Christ-like to them."

The next morning Patrick woke before dawn and drove the sheep out to the mountain. He needed comfort from his loving heavenly Father. Worshiping the Lord always put everything into proper perspective. He could always count on the Lord to be with him: when taking care of the sheep, when sleeping in the dirty sheepfold, in bad weather, even when others persecuted him and made fun of him. Patrick knew God's protection upon him. Only when he spent time praying to God and receiving nourishment from God did he then have the strength to comfort others with the love of Christ.

Even despite his miserable circumstances, Patrick knew that ultimately his soul was secure in Christ. He had the hope of heaven, being able to spend eternity with the Lord. It was this hope that kept him going.

How he loved to be alone on the mountain, for there he was alone with his Savior! "Lord, you are more precious to me than gold! Nothing I desire compares to you!" Patrick found in Christ a friend that sticks closer than a brother. He knew Christ truly loved him, had compassion on him, provided for him, protected him, comforted, and guided him.

Everything Patrick had cherished as a selfish child held no value to him anymore. All the riches of his father's villa meant nothing to him. His status as a Roman decurion's son was meaningless. He was a true child of God, the Almighty God, the Creator of the Universe. He had forgiveness of sins from the Savior of the world.

As Patrick walked along the hedge, he spied Berach helping Aelric working in the fields.

"Here comes our holy boy!" Aelric taunted, spying Patrick's approach. Berach started laughing. "How many times did you pray to your God today?"

Patrick just smiled. He didn't mind their teasing now. He knew that this was their own strange way of showing their affection for him. He also knew it was hard for Aelric and Berach to understand Patrick's unique communion with his Heavenly Father. They couldn't fathom how Patrick could spend countless hours up on the mountain in "rambling devotion" to his God.

"How's that leg of yours?" Patrick asked Berach.

"Doing well," Berach replied quietly, silenced from his laughing at the reminder of how his life had been miraculously saved, still to everyone's amazement.

Patrick left Aelric and Berach and continued to drive the sheep out to their pastures below the mountain.

Every day Patrick would spend hours in prayer up on the mountain. He loved praying to his Father in heaven and meditating upon the word that the Lord would bring to his mind. Some days he would pray up to one hundred times a day and would even pray through the night!

Patrick could also sense the love of God growing within him. The more time he spent out on the mountain, in union with Christ, the more he could feel God's love for him. He felt so loved and alive like he had never felt before. He was a lowly, vile slave, a fudir, and yet he was loved by the Lord God Almighty, the King of Kings! And slowly, Patrick's hatred for the Irish began to die, and he began to develop a love for them.

The more time he spent with the Lord, and the more time he met in worship with the other Christians, the Lord began to open Patrick's mind and heart to the Scriptures. Through his suffering he began to know the Scriptures at a very deep level. He recalled the many times he would spend memorizing the word of God under his grandfather's watchful eye. He had such a hunger for the word now, and the word filled the longing in his heart.

"Oh, how I wish I had memorized more," Patrick thought to himself. Feeling ashamed for how dull he had been as a child, and how cold he had been in his love for Christ, Patrick resolved to pray and meditate upon the word even more.

"How could I serve God more?" Patrick wondered. "Lord, I know you brought me here for a purpose. I know you brought me here to humble me and bring me to yourself. But I can't help thinking that you did all that to just have me tend sheep my whole life."

Patrick continued thinking as he made his way to the clearing, a place he had come to love with all his heart. The little group of Christian slaves that met for worship had become very dear to Patrick. The group had also grown as the change in Patrick's life brought curious visitors to the services who wanted to see this "holy boy".

He loved singing the hymns with gusto. It was very important to be able to fellowship with other believers. Patrick had even started to take on more of a leadership role within the group. Killian had noticed the natural gift Patrick had for leadership and encouraged him to pray and quote the scriptures he knew by heart.

"Patrick," Killian cleared his throat. "You are the only one of us who has had any formal education. I believe God is going to use you mightily. God has great things in store for you."

Hearing Killian say this made Patrick very excited. It was as if God was confirming to Patrick what he had been thinking. Suddenly a thought came into Patrick's mind. "I know—I could write down all the scripture we know between all of us. We would then have a written copy to use in our worship services!"

"That would be wonderful," Killian had stated. "But the only person who has parchment would be Odhrain."

"Leave that problem to me," Patrick said, his mind racing. He hadn't noticed Bain slipping away from behind a Rowan tree.

"I warned you about the prophecy," Odhrain hissed to Miliucc. "It is coming true right before our very eyes. That Roman boy is the one who will try to convert our land. He needs to be stopped!"

61

"But I have never known such prosperity since he has come to me," Miliucc countered.

"He defies our gods," Odhrain said scornfully. "He even wants to put the writings of this Father God onto parchment so he can spread its filthy lies across our rath—and entire kingdom!"

Filled with rage, Odhrain left the main hall with his raven screeching. "Gosact will have more sense!"

Odhrain found Gosact in the stable about to mount his horse. "Gosact, what I have to discuss with you is very important!"

"I'm listening," replied Gosact, interested.

"That Roman slave boy is a threat to our people. He must be killed."

"I don't want to betray my father, but I agree," Gosact said. "Leave the matter with me. In the morning, he will be no more."

Chapter 16

Escape

That same night Patrick lay awake too excited to sleep. He was trying to think of how he could get parchment from Odhrain. The thought of writing down scripture to be used in the worship of God thrilled his soul. He had been up on the mountain all afternoon and evening, praying and fasting. He felt the Spirit's lead as he prayed. "Oh, Lord, continue to have mercy upon your servant. Grant me your wisdom and guidance. Show me your will, Lord. You know I want to do great things for you."

As he prayed and meditated on scripture, Patrick seemed to hear the Holy Spirit speaking to his spirit. "You do well to fast. Soon you will depart for your home country. Your ship is ready. Make your way to the sea."

Patrick sat up with a start. God's voice had come to him so stark and clear. This was not what he was expecting. The Lord was telling him to leave his master and to find a ship that was waiting for him.

"Thank you, Lord, for answering my prayer so quickly."

Grabbing his blackthorn staff, Patrick wasted no time in making his way down the mountain. This would be the last time he would make the well- known journey down the rocky slopes of Slemish to the little sheepfold. The moonlight cast an eerie glow on the purple heather plants clinging to the massive mountain.

He was twenty-two now and had worked for Miliucc for six long, hard years. The mountain was his home. The little group of slaves that gathered for worship in the wood was now his family.

Patrick looked at the sheep huddled in the fold. He had grown quite fond of the sheep entrusted to his care. For the last six years his whole life had revolved around sheep. Patrick felt a certain regret for abandoning them. But he knew that God would take care of them.

He also felt a pang of regret for leaving Miliucc. As a Christian he had to obey his master. But his first priority was to obey his heavenly Master. He also knew that he, as a runaway slave, would be blamed for any failure or trouble that would come upon Miliucc's sheep herd. Patrick knew that Miliucc attributed the success of his crops and livestock to himself. Since becoming a Christian Patrick had tried with the best of his ability and God's strength to work for Miliucc as honestly and obediently as he could. But Miliucc still did not believe that it was the one true God working through Patrick who brought blessing.

The thought of leaving his little family of fellow believers saddened him most of all. He loved Killian like a brother and felt bad about not keeping his promise to write down the scriptures for the believers. Of all people, though, he knew Killian would understand. Killian would want Patrick to obey God no matter what.

Patrick knelt on the trampled dirt inside the sheepfold and prayed to God. "Oh, heavenly Father, lead me and guide me and show me your way. Keep me safe and help me to do your will. Give me the strength to carry out your will that you have so clearly shown to me."

Without a moment's hesitation, Patrick took off with complete trust in God. He was used to hardship, and nothing, not even fleeing from his master, would stop him from obeying God. His life was Christ's to do with whatever the Lord wanted to do. He could hear the words loud and clear that the Spirit had spoken to him. Not even fear would hold him back. Patrick knew that God would lead him and take care of him.

Slipping through the back gate of the fort, Patrick made his way to one of the storage buildings, walking as quietly as he could to not wake up the hounds. He grabbed some bread and cheese, stuffed them into a cloth, and grabbed a skein of water, being careful to only take what would have been given to him to eat that day. He looked over at the slave hut where Aelric and Berach were sound asleep. Patrick thought for a moment of waking them but decided against it. He didn't want to put them in an awkward situation. Better that they didn't know. He didn't want to create a scene and, worse, wouldn't want them to be punished on account of him.

Dropping a few pieces of bread to the waking hounds, Patrick was able to slip back through the gate unnoticed. He would travel by night and try to find places to rest during the day. He knew the danger of being a runaway slave and wondered how long it would be before Miliucc would send people out looking for him. And there was also the danger of being captured by someone else. He would have to travel through unknown lands, through rival tuaths.

"Oh God, help me to trust you. Take away my fear," Patrick prayed. He felt like Abraham when God told him to set out for a new land. He didn't know where he was going, but he was trusting God to lead him.

Excitement and adrenaline were making his heart pound within his chest. With his blackthorn staff in his hand, Patrick closed the back gate of the rath for the last time. He recollected the first day he had made the journey to Miliucc's fort, Gosact pulling him with a rope tied around his neck. He had been so stubborn, hard-hearted, and bitter. God had changed him so drastically. Patrick laughed to himself, thinking that now he had mixed feelings about leaving a place he had once so hated. He marveled at the love of God, how it could change such a hard heart and soften it, enabling someone to care not for his own concerns and comforts, but desire to be poured out in love for one's enemies.

Patrick took one final glance at the rath of Miliucc and started down the long path through the Irish countryside. He turned his back on the life of slavery he had lived for six long, hard years. He couldn't wait to see what God had in store for him. The excitement was just too much. He felt like shouting for joy, but he dared not. He didn't want Gosact and his warriors at his heels sooner than later.

Chapter 17

Journey Through the Night

After journeying all through the night, Patrick came across a field of haystacks. He picked one close to the edge of a wood, far from the path, and crawled inside so he wouldn't be seen. "Thank you, Lord, for guiding me here and providing this place of shelter. You are my refuge, an ever, present help in times of trouble."

Patrick pushed away the hay from around him to make a nest he could burrow into and sleep. Looking down at his hands, he noticed they were now rough and scarred, but they were strong. No longer the hands of a Roman noble's son. He ran his finger over the scar on the back of his right hand. When it rained, which was a lot, the scar still hurt. A wolf had tried to snatch a baby lamb a year ago, and Patrick had fought the wolf and eventually killed it.

Shifting in the scratchy hay to get comfortable, Patrick thought about how he had changed in many ways. He still marveled at the changes God had inflicted upon his heart. Not only was he a man now, but he was a person reborn. He loved God with all his heart, mind, soul, and strength. He had learned how to be in constant communion with his heavenly Father in prayer. Being totally dependent upon Christ, he had learned to be led by the Spirit, always listening to the Spirit's voice. God had taken a proud, angry, dirty, rotten heart and poured his love and grace into it, giving him a soft and humble heart full of love and compassion in return.

With his blackthorn stick by his side, Patrick drifted into a deep sleep. The cares of his life having been laid to rest with his heavenly Father, Patrick slept content and at peace, unaware of the activity of the day all around him.

Back at Miliucc's fort, dawn was met with Odhrain letting out a blood curdling cry. Gosact wasted no time in mounting his stallion. In a furious rage he and several of his warriors galloped off down the path searching for Patrick, their swords drawn.

At dusk Patrick woke, ate some bread and cheese, and peeked out of the hay. The sun was just starting to set. There was no one in sight. Not wanting to linger, Patrick decided he should set out on the road again. He still had a long journey ahead of him. Patrick was glad there was a forest lining the left side of the road. He could take cover if he heard someone approaching. After saying a prayer, he climbed out of his nest and started walking again, trusting God would protect him and bring him safely to the harbor.

The night was crisp and clear. As he walked Patrick found himself thinking about Lupita. He had heard nothing of her in the last six years. Was she still alive? Should he even dare to ask about her? If he did, he might give himself away. Patrick still worried greatly for his sister but trusted the Lord for her. He had given her safety and, even more importantly her salvation, over to the Lord. Patrick knew that God would watch over Lupita and care for her in his perfect and pleasing way. Just like God had brought Patrick to Ireland to humble him and draw him to Himself, he was confident and prayed that God would be doing the same for Lupita. He no more prayed that God would provide a way of escape for Lupita. He now prayed that Lupita would not resist God's dealings in her life, that she would not grow bitter towards God, and that she would trust in God as her heavenly Father.

His feet aching from walking all night, Patrick started looking for a place to hide and rest for the day. Sunlight was now beginning to come up over the horizon. He was able to pray while he rested, which gave him comfort. Keeping in constant communion with God sustained him and gave him strength to keep going. Patrick's practice of fasting much had prepared him for being able to go without food for long periods of time. He never felt alone for the Lord was always with him.

So far there had been no sign of Gosact. Patrick wasn't sure which tuath he was travelling through now. Seeing signs of a fort nearby he had to find a place to hide fast. There was a forest on the far end of the field he was walking along side of. He would have to cross the field and slip into the woods.

Thankfully the grass in the field was high. Hearing voices, Patrick jumped into the grass and lay down to conceal himself. The voices came closer.

"Tiarnan, have you seen any strange youths about the woods or fields?" a man asked.

"No, Ruairi, I have not," said the other.

"Chief Miliucc's son, from the neighboring tuath north of here, came by with some of his warriors yesterday. Said he was after one of his runaway slaves," Ruairi said. "Keep a look out for him. He would bring a nice reward. Miliucc would pay a nice price."

After making sure the two men were well away, Patrick poked his head up through the grass. Seeing no one about, he crawled through the grass on his belly to the edge of the field. Walking a short distance into the forest, he spied a small cave and claimed it for his hideout.

"Oh, thank you Lord, for keeping me safe," he prayed. "And thank you for revealing to me the information about Gosact."

After two weeks of travelling by night and scrounging for food wherever he could find it, Patrick began to smell the salty sea air. He could hear the cries of the gulls circling the shore. Pretty soon he could hear the crashing of the waves and the shouts of men loading and unloading cargo.

Patrick found himself at a port on the south east coast. He knelt and praised God for bringing him safe and sound and for guiding him the whole way. "Thank you, Lord, for showing me the way to go, and for keeping me safe."

Chapter 18

Captain and Crew

P atrick spied a fisherman's hut nestled into a bluff overlooking the shore. A man was sitting outside the hut, propped up against his curragh, mending his nets. Grey smoke rose out of a cackling fire in the center of a circle of rocks.

"Do you mind if I warm myself by your fire?" Patrick asked kindly.

The old fisherman nodded toward the fire as his bony fingers wrestled with a ripped net. He kept a suspicious eye on Patrick.

"Is there any work here?" Patrick asked, sensing he was safe from danger here.

"Plenty of work," the man spoke through his greying beard. "But be careful they don't make you a slave." He gestured to the sailors busy working around the ships in the harbor below.

"Thank you for the warmth of you fire," Patrick said.

The port was crowded with four ships anchored at its docks. As Patrick walked closer his eye caught a certain ship that was almost ready to set sail. He watched the sailors working with their cargo, some Irish wolfhounds, which were barking incessantly. Seeing the wolfhounds reminded Patrick of his own dog, Maxi, back home.

Feeling the Spirit's lead, Patrick confidently walked over to one of the crew. When the hounds on deck saw Patrick, they immediately stopped barking and struggling with the crew.

The ship was already untied from its moorings, and the anchor was just being raised when Patrick called out. "Do you have room to take on another man?" Patrick asked the rough looking sailor. "I have no money, but I work hard."

The sailor yelled up to his captain who had been looking on from the deck. "Hey, Captain Gahrban, this boy wants passage. Says he'll work hard."

"He's probably a runaway slave, Fearghal. He'll bring bad luck," the captain shouted down angrily from the deck, "No way! He won't go with us!" Patrick nodded respectfully and started to walk away, praying as he went.

"Oh, Lord, I know this is the ship you have prepared for me. Please help me. Show me what to do."

The captain watched Patrick. "This man is different," he thought. "There is something about his manner. He doesn't act like a typical runaway. Strangely, the dogs are even better behaved with him around." Doubting himself, he began to wonder, "If I refuse him, I might have bad luck."

Patrick didn't get very far when one of the crew called for Patrick to come back. "Come quickly because the captain is calling you."

As the boat slipped away from the shore, Patrick watched the land of his enslavement slowly fade away into the distance.

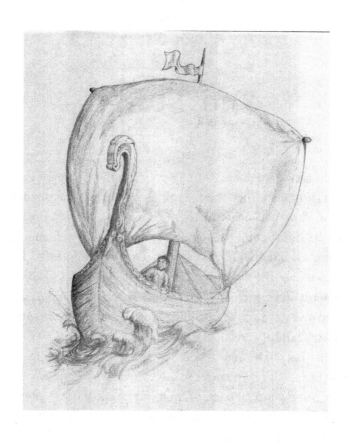

Chapter 19

The Storm

The crew Patrick was sailing with was hoping to reach southern Gaul where they were going to trade their Irish hounds to wealthy villa owners. After dealing with Gosact, life among the sailors didn't come as a complete shock. They were rough, but Patrick worked hard, didn't complain, and kept to himself as much as he could aboard the ship. The sailors made Patrick take care of the hounds since the dogs behaved so well with him. As Patrick watched over the dogs, he imagined himself taking care of Maxi and his father's hunting dogs.

Below deck, the lanky hounds lay curled up at Patrick's feet. They slept as he spent time in prayer. "Father, thank you for preserving my life and helping me to escape. Thank you for showing me the way to go. Help me to stay faithful to you and to be obedient to you. Help me to be content in all circumstances and not to complain. Thank you for bringing these sailors into my life and help me to show Christ to them." He reached down and stroked the head of a hound resting his head on his knee. Sitting there in the dirty straw on the floor, with the hounds around him, Patrick wondered what God had in store for him next.

Up on deck the sailors were discussing their plans. "These hounds will bring a pretty penny in Gaul," Fearghal stated. "I say we also sell the lad, too," he added with a smile.

"It's tempting," the captain said, "but we will keep him. We will make him work for us. He is good for our hound trade, very useful with the dogs. He will bring us good luck."

For three days the tiny ship sailed. Patrick was sleeping when he was wakened suddenly by being thrown against a beam, one of the ribs of the ship's hull. "Ow!" he groaned, rubbing his side. He slowly made it to a kneeling position, expecting to see Fearghal towering over him, ready to beat him for whatever reason. But the ship pitched again, sending Patrick tumbling back to where he had been sleeping.

The quaking hounds watched Patrick with frightful eyes. Holding on to the dogs' ropes to steady himself, he made sure they were fastened securely. "It's all right boys," Patrick consoled them as they whimpered in protest of the storm. "God will keep us safe."

It seemed like an eternity had passed when Patrick finally felt the ship's rocking start to ease. It had been a rough night, holding tight to one of the ropes, while he and the dogs slid across the floor and back again. After being up all night, it was easy for Patrick to let himself be lulled to sleep by the now gentle rocking of the boat.

Chapter 20

Gaul

Patrick was jolted awake by the sound of the hatch above him creaking open. The sound of the sailors scrambling about was loud and clear.

"Hey, boy, get the hounds ready. We're going ashore," one of the sailors grunted.

The crew cast anchor and began to make ready. Patrick held the hounds' rope with a tight grip. Even he could not keep them quiet as everyone was anxious to get onto dry land again.

It was all Patrick could do to keep the hounds from pulling him into the water. "Steady, boys." The waves slapping at his legs, he could feel the cold wet sea surround his feet as he stepped into the surf.

Once on shore, Captain Gahrban began barking orders to the other sailors. Fearghal came up behind Patrick and shoved him forward with the side of his sword. "Move!" he shouted. "I'm watching you. You try to run for it, and you will meet my blade."

The sailors were exhausted after fighting the storm all night. And they were angry and frustrated, too, because the storm had driven them off course. They weren't sure where in Gaul they had landed.

Their journey took them through what looked like a wasteland. Patrick couldn't believe the desolation. The crew marched on in silence as they looked out at the fields and farms that were devastated by all the destruction. Patrick's heart ached as he viewed what was left of villas torn apart by war.

"Keep a close look out," Gahrban grunted to the crew. "Looks like the Vandals have been through here, forcing the Romans to withdraw."

Mention of the Romans got Patrick's attention. He couldn't believe the Roman army would be beaten back so much. So much had changed in the world, the civilized world, since he had been a slave in Ireland. "What is Britain going to be like?" he wondered.

"We had better keep off the roads," Gahrban motioned to the other sailors. Swords drawn, they crept slowly through the brush.

Fearghal kept his blade close to Patrick's back. "You had better keep those dogs quiet!" he hissed.

Chapter 21

Barbarians

After marching for a few hours, the company stopped for a rest. Patrick quietly prayed to the Lord while keeping the hounds calm. He spoke quietly to each one, knowing their personalities well now.

Without any warning, one of the sailors thudded to the ground, an arrow sticking out from his chest. Another arrow hit the trunk of the tree Patrick was sitting against. He immediately threw himself down on the ground. The hounds started barking and straining at their ropes, the hair on the back of their necks raised.

"Barbarians!" Gahrban shouted. "Stay low." Patrick pulled some brush over himself as the sailors tried to find cover.

Patrick could hear his own heart thumping inside his chest. He didn't dare lift his head for fear of giving himself away or making a sound. "Oh Lord," he prayed, "please preserve us, if it be your will."

He suddenly felt a tight grip on his arm pulling him out of his cover. Fearghal pressed his scarred face close. "I told you to stay close," he hissed. Fearghal then raised his sword and swung it down on the ropes holding back the anxious dogs. "Go, attack!" the sailor shouted at them as the dogs took off running toward the Barbarians at top speed.

"No!" Patrick cried, forgetting about trying to stay safe.

Fearghal slapped him across the face. "Be quiet!" he commanded, grabbing the ropes and shoving Patrick against a tree. He quickly tied Patrick tight to the tree, and then ran off to join the sailors in pursuit of the Barbarians.

Patrick wriggled as hard as he could, trying to free himself of his bonds. But the ropes just dug into him and he couldn't budge. He could do nothing but pray. Even in the midst of the terror he could sense the powerful presence of the Holy Spirit giving him peace. He could hear the screams of men and their swords clashing as the fight was now hand to hand. The hounds had found their target.

The fight was short lived, and Patrick soon saw the sailors making their way back to him. The hounds ran right to Patrick and started sniffing him, curious about the ropes holding him to the tree.

Only Gahrban, Fearghal, and three others returned. "We had better get moving again," the captain grunted. Gahrban wiped his sword against his trousers. "Get the boy and let's go." Patrick was roughly unstrapped from the tree and again he found Fearghal's blade pressed against his back.

"Father, thank you for preserving me again," Patrick prayed silently. "Please give me strength to keep living for you. And bring me to my home."

Chapter 22

God Provides

Patrick and the crew started journeying again through the wasteland. He tried to imagine what the countryside would have looked like before the Vandals came and the Romans were driven out. "These were once farms just like in Britain," Patrick thought. "I wonder what my father's villa will be like when I get there."

"We are getting nowhere," one of the crew complained.

"Yeah, we're starving, too," one of the other sailors joined in the complaining. "We haven't eaten in days."

"We need to trust God. He will show us the way," Patrick said.

"Shut up!" Gahrban shouted. "No one asked you." The crew laughed.

Patrick knew he could always pray quietly, despite the taunts and teasing. "Oh, Lord, please show us the way to go. Lead us to civilization, to people."

They seemed to march for days. Patrick's gut was gnawing at him with hunger. All means of trying to hunt for food had been hopeless. Even the dogs were showing signs of exhaustion, growing weaker and weaker.

Sadly, the crew had to resort to eating the wolf hounds. Patrick fought back tears; he was devastated but knew it had to be done. Providentially, he knew that this was God's way of keeping them all alive.

The sailors grew more frustrated with having to eat the dogs, losing their profit. This made their tempers worse and Fearghal treated Patrick more harshly. "This is all your fault!" he hissed at Patrick as they stopped for a rest. "You bring nothing but bad luck."

Patrick tried to ignore Fearghal's insults. He closed his eyes and started to pray to the Lord.

"Right, we need to get moving again," the captain shouted. The men mustered their strength, moaning, as they tried to make their weary bodies stand.

As Patrick was getting up from praying to the Lord, he felt something cold and sharp press against his throat. Fearghal had grabbed Patrick from behind and was holding a knife to his throat.

"I say we kill him," the first mate snarled. "We don't need any extra mouths to feed. We don't need him anymore."

Gahrban looked over at Patrick held captive by a wild eyed Fearghal. "Now, Christian, you say that your God is great and almighty. Why don't you pray to Him for us? We are in danger of starvation and there is little chance we will come upon help."

Still feeling the cool blade pressing against his neck and Fearghal's strong arm across his chest, Patrick tried to show no fear. Having complete confidence in God he replied, "Nothing is impossible for the Lord, my God."

Patrick then looked toward heaven and started to pray. "Oh Lord, my complete trust is in you, my Lord and my God. I turn to you with all my heart and ask that you may send us food in our path this day until we are filled, for you have plenty in all places."

No sooner than Patrick had finished the last words of his prayer, noises were heard coming from the brush along the side of the road. Then to the sailors' amazement, a drove of pigs appeared out from the brush and wandered within a few yards of the shocked and famished group.

Patrick felt Fearghal let him go. While the sailors killed many of the pigs, Patrick bowed low to the ground and thanked the Lord for rescuing him and answering his prayer.

After the slaughter was over, all eyes turned to Patrick. "God has been merciful to us," Patrick said. "You should put your trust in him, the God who made the world and rules over everything."

"This God, He is the one true God, who made heaven and earth, and all that is in the earth. He made you all," Patrick went on. "The one true God is our heavenly Father who not only made us but loves us. He even sent his own Son, Jesus Christ, to come to earth and die for those who would believe in him. And God the Father promises that if we confess our sin, are truly sorry for our sin, he will forgive us and give us eternal life." Patrick said this, looking Fearghal right in the face. The hard man just turned his eyes away.

While the crew made fires to roast the meat, one of the sailors came back to the camp very excited. "Look what I've found!" he exclaimed, his sticky hands holding onto a hive oozing with honey. "The gods have found favor with us again." The sailor approached Patrick with an outstretched arm. "Here, take it as a sacrifice."

Patrick looked at the sweet honey, his mouth watering. It had been a long time since he had tasted honey. But he would not eat something that was to be given up in a pagan ritual. "Thank you, but no," he said. "But I will pray to God and give him thanks for providing us with this bountiful food."

They rested in that place for two nights. Patrick noticed that the sailors weren't as rough with him now and didn't make fun of him when he prayed.

As Patrick slept, his belly satisfied with a feed of ham, he fell into a deep dream. He dreamed that a great stone fell on top of him, crushing his chest. He struggled but couldn't move his arms and legs. He thrashed about but the stone would not budge. Then he sensed a heavy darkness descend upon him, surrounding him. It was all he could do to take a breath, his lungs seeming to fill with the icy darkness, suffocating him every time he sucked in air.

Before it was too late, he forced out one final gasp, "Oh God, help me!" he cried. As he called to the Lord the beams of the rising sun woke him. Slowly the crushing heaviness began to fade away and his breath came to him again. Patrick sat up and wiped the sweat from his dripping brow.

"This was not just a nightmare," Patrick wondered. The realization that the evil one himself had been tempting him with despair hit him hard. But with the morning sun he knew that Christ had come to strengthen and encourage him. Patrick was beginning to realize that the evil one will try even harder to bring down those who walk closely with the Lord. But he also knew that Christ was always there to provide help.

Nine more days Patrick and his companions travelled through Gaul. They came upon a large river and decided to follow it, hoping to find civilization. On the tenth day they finally encountered other men.

A group of five monks dressed in their long, brown robes were sitting in a cluster off the side of the road, near the river. They were singing a prayer in Latin as they cooked some fish over a fire.

The smell of the frying fish came wafting through the air to Patrick's nostrils. He stepped cautiously forward, motioning the rest of the crew to hang back. Trying to remember his Latin, Patrick timidly approached the group of monks.

"Excuse me fathers," Patrick began. The startled monks looked up from their fish to see Patrick standing there in front of them. They then spied the motley crew of sailors and terror began to take over their faces.

"It's okay. Don't be afraid," Patrick assured them. "We seek you no harm. We were shipwrecked and are lost. Can you help us?"

One of the monks stood up but still glanced suspiciously at the sailors. Patrick called over to Gahrban, "Throw your weapons down. They need to trust us." Reluctantly Gahrban instructed his men to disarm themselves, and the sailors begrudgingly laid their weapons in a pile on the ground.

A little more satisfied, the standing monk walked closer to Patrick and introduced himself.

"I am Father Vincentius," the man said, "from the abbey at Lerins. My brothers and I are traveling to Tours to help with some teaching," Vincentius commented as he motioned towards his fellow companions.

At the mention of Tours, Patrick spoke excitedly to Vicentius. "How far away is Tours?" he asked.

"Only half a day's journey following the river," Vincentius nodded and pointed east.

Patrick took this news back to Gahrban and his crew who were waiting anxiously.

"Tell the monk we will protect them if they get us to Tours," the captain said.

Patrick relayed the message back to Vincentius and Vincentius motioned the men over. "Come and eat," he said.

Patrick could hardly eat anything with the excitement of Tours being so close. Tours was the home of his uncle, his mother's brother, Martin, bishop of Tours.

Chapter 23

Uncle Martin

Patrick chatted with Vincentius as the group of sailors and monks walked the road along the shore of the Loire River. Patrick recounted to Vincentius all that had happened to him. The monk listened eagerly with fascination as Patrick told of his kidnapping by Irish raiders, becoming a slave, and of his escape. Vincentius was amazed as Patrick shared his testimony of how God had saved him and changed his life.

As they walked along, Patrick was so engrossed in conversation with Vincentius that he hadn't noticed the change in their surroundings. They had long ago left the dense brush of the forests, and now the quiet serenity of the river and fields of grape vines gave the travelers pleasant scenery to admire. Soon they found themselves on a bustling street lined by crude huts. Patrick nearly escaped collision with an overflowing cart of vegetables being pushed by a man along the busy street.

Fearghal grabbed Patrick and pulled him off to the side of the road. This time Patrick was glad of the strong grip from the rough sailor.

"This is where we leave you," Captain Gahrban said to Patrick. "We know of some contacts here who might be able to help us."

"God be with you," Patrick said.

Fearghal let Patrick go. "Remember me in your prayers," he asked gruffly.

"I promise," Patrick replied with a warm smile. Fearghal merely nodded to Patrick and the sailors turned and went on their own way.

"Now, we need to find your uncle," said Vincentius. "He will most likely be at his monastery, Marmoutier."

Patrick was amused as he thought about how he had so quickly changed company from a group of fighting sailors to a band of peaceful monks. His new friends led him through the center of Tours. They passed a huge amphitheater with rows and rows of circular stone seats that descended to a stage in the middle.

"Your uncle's monastery is on the other side of the river," Vincentius mentioned to Patrick.

The group made their way to a path that led out of the city center, down to the edge of the river. Small boats were docked, ready to ferry people across.

Soon Patrick and his friends came to his uncle's monastery. A stone church with a simple wooden steeple rising from the center of the roof was encircled by several other smaller buildings. The church reminded Patrick of the church in Bannavem where his grandfather was a priest.

Patrick, Vincentius, and the band of monks approached the oak door, and Vincentius knocked on the door with the iron door knocker. After a few moments they could hear footsteps getting nearer, and then a voice called out.

"Who's there?" asked a raspy voice from inside.

"Father Vincentius has come to see Bishop Martin," Vincentius called back in reply.

The wooden doors scraped open a crack and the visitors could see an old face peering out. At the sight of the monks, the old priest opened the doors wider so the group could venture in.

"Yes, good afternoon, brothers. We are expecting you," the aged man said. "I am Brother Franco."

"Thank you, Brother Franco," Vincentius said, smiling to the old man. Patrick and the monks walked into the dark vestibule and gathered near a small table holding some candles. Brother Franco, already holding a candle, motioned with his shaky hand for the visitors to follow him.

Brother Franco led the group through the sanctuary. It felt good for Patrick to be back inside a Christian place of worship. This was his first time being in a church and appreciating it. He wanted to sit down in one of the pews and worship God right then and there. Feeling his heart starting to well up with praise, tears started running down Patrick's cheeks as the wooden cross on the wall behind the pulpit came into view. It was all Patrick could do to make himself leave the sanctuary and keep following the group of monks.

They were led down a short corridor lined with wooden doors on each side. Brother Franco stopped at a door at the end of the corridor and knocked on it with his bony knuckles. "Excuse me, Bishop, Father Vincentius and some guests are here to see you."

"Let them in," a voice from inside the door said.

Brother Franco opened the door and then turned to leave.

Patrick stared at the big man sitting behind a wooden desk. His uncle! He realized that this was the first time in a little over six years he had seen someone from his family. The vivid resemblance of his mother in the man's features was too much for Patrick to bear.

"Father Vincentius, welcome," Bishop Martin said as he stood up behind the desk. "I trust you had safe travels. I look forward to talking with you about your writings and sitting in on your lectures."

"Thank you, Bishop. Yes, God has granted us a safe journey from Lerins. And I am excited and honored about the opportunity to teach here at the monastery."

"Good, good. Brother Franco outside will show you where you are to stay, and there will be some food and drink made ready."

Patrick was getting impatient with all the formalities. He wanted to cry out to his uncle. He realized his uncle didn't recognize him. "My uncle probably thinks I am dead or still a slave in Ireland, and that he will never see me again," Patrick wondered.

"Thank you, Bishop," Vincentius went on, and as if to read Patrick's mind he added, "but we also have with us a friend whom I am sure you will be most happy to be reacquainted with again." Vincentius looked at Patrick and with a wink nodded for him to come forward.

"Hello, Uncle," Patrick said, hardly able to contain himself from flinging himself at the big man.

The shocked bishop stared in awe at the young man before him, his jaw dropping. "No, it can't be!" Martin reached out his hands, holding Patrick's face. "It is you, Patrick!"

With tears streaming down both their faces, Martin and Patrick clung to each other in one long embrace. After a while, when their sobbing had subsided, Martin pulled himself away a short distance and grasped Patrick's shoulders with his hands.

"Well, let me have a good look at you," Martin said quietly. Vincentius and the others had quietly and respectfully left the room, letting Brother Franco show them to their rooms.

"I was afraid you would not know me, Uncle," Patrick admitted bashfully.

"I thought I would never see you again," Martin said. When I got news of what had happened," Martin paused, fighting for words. "Your mother told me what happened to your poor grandfather."

Martin looked at Patrick's face again. "When I saw your eyes, I knew it was you," Martin said. "You have your mother's eyes." He looked away sadly.

"How are my mother and father?" Patrick asked excitedly.

"Patrick, I have much to tell you. But first, you must be famished and exhausted. I'll show you to your room, you can get refreshed, and then you and I will talk over supper."

Chapter 24

Family

Patrick immediately flung himself down on the bed in the room. It had been over six whole years since he had lain on a bed. Sinking down into the mattress, he wrapped the soft sheets around him, and slept like he had never slept before.

When he woke, it was dark outside. After bathing he found the clothes that were laid out for him. The fresh, clean tunic felt so good. It had been a long time since Patrick had put on new, clean garments. He felt like a new person.

Patrick descended a stone stairwell to a small dining hall where his uncle waited for him. Sitting down in his seat, Patrick watched his uncle slice his meat with a knife. He had only met his uncle a few times but had always admired him. Many years ago, his Uncle Martin had been a Roman officer, before becoming a bishop. Patrick had enjoyed hearing his stories of the army.

"Patrick," Martin began. "Now I must tell you about your parents."

Patrick braced himself as his uncle continued. "Your mother is not well." Martin looked at Patrick with solemn eyes. "When she and your father returned after that awful night … the night they took you … the night your grandfather died… well, it took a lot out of her. She has been failing ever since."

Patrick slowly took in what his uncle was saying to him. It felt strange to be talking about his parents. It had been so long, and he was so different. He hadn't really thought about the fact that they would be different, too. He still imagined them as they were when he was a sixteen- year old boy, his mother so elegant and beautiful.

"What about my father?" Patrick asked nervously.

"Your father is alive. And he is as hard as ever, I'm sad to say." Patrick nodded his head silently. He had been praying for his father ever since his own salvation. He had been praying that his father's heart would not be hardened even more by the circumstances of that dreadful night.

"You know that although the Lord used me to win my mother to Christ, I could not persuade my father to become a Christian," Martin said to Patrick with sympathy in his voice. "There is always hope. We must keep praying."

Patrick remembered hearing his mother tell him the story of his heroic uncle who crossed the Alps, and from Milan went over to Pannonia, to give his parents the gospel. "Did God take me all the way to Ireland and bring me back to convert my father?" he wondered.

As a boy, Patrick had always thought of his Uncle Martin as bigger than life. His mother admired her brother and had the utmost respect for him. Patrick's father thought he was insane, throwing away a bright and promising military career just to become a priest. Patrick wondered what his father would think of his own conversion and love for the Lord.

"Your parents sent word to me of what had happened," Martin continued. "I never prayed like I prayed in those days, Patrick. I have been praying for your safety and, of course your salvation. And God has answered my prayers on both accounts. Here you are now."

Patrick and Martin ate in silence for a moment. Patrick tried to process all that his uncle had just shared with him. Then Martin broke the silence.

"Patrick, have you any information about Lupita?"

"Nothing, Uncle. The last time I saw her was on the night we were taken." Patrick swallowed hard. "It's like she just disappeared. I kept my eyes out for her all the time, at the markets and festivals, everywhere. I asked around about her, too. I asked travellers and other slaves, but no one had heard anything about her. Ireland is such a big country, a vast wilderness."

"We must keep praying for her, then. Nothing is impossible for God. Here you are after praying for six, long years! And look at all God has brought you through!" Martin smiled at Patrick. "Oh, what does God have in store for you, Patrick?"

Chapter 25

Time to Go

The next morning Patrick couldn't wait to go back to the sanctuary. He was the first one there, eagerly waiting to worship the Lord. After living so long in a land that was immersed in paganism and where there was no formal Christian worship, Patrick was bursting with excitement to be able to worship the Lord in an actual worship service in a real church.

After a prayer, Martin introduced Vincentius, who would be giving a series of lectures to the monks. As Patrick worshipped, he thought of Killian and the small group that worshipped in the wood of Fochlad.

Patrick thoroughly enjoyed his time at Tours, being able to rest and become "civilized" again. Vincentius was a gifted teacher and Patrick appreciated being able to sit in on some of his lectures. But he especially enjoyed being able to spend time with his uncle. Uncle Martin was someone he could empathize with. It was such a blessing having someone he could talk feely with about the Lord. Patrick imagined that the way he talked with his uncle was what it would have been like if he could have talked with his grandfather.

Martin seemed to know how Patrick thought, and what he was feeling, having been through dramatic experiences in his life as well. Patrick found a kindred spirit in his uncle. They both knew what it was to live a life in close communion with the Lord. God had used the dramatic events in Martin's life to bring great service to the Lord and his church. Patrick valued this time spent with his uncle and asked his advice on everything he could think of.

He could listen to his uncle tell stories and give advice all day. One story Martin told Patrick about was an incident that happened when he was a soldier in the Roman army deployed in Gaul. One day as he was approaching the gates of the city of Amiens, he met a scantily clad beggar. Martin impulsively cut his military cloak in half and gave one half to the man. That night in his dream, Martin saw Jesus wearing the half-cloak he had given away.

"I heard Jesus say to the angels in heaven, 'Martin, who is still but a catechumen, clothed me with this robe.' When I woke, Patrick, I vowed I would do all I could to help those in need, primarily to give the gospel!"

"Uncle, I have dreams, sometimes, too!" Patrick admitted excitedly.

"Just remember, Patrick, that God speaks to us primarily through his word. Only his word will keep you on the right path. You have a brilliant mind. Learn as much of the scriptures as you can."

Martin continued, "when I was converted to Christ, I found my new faith incompatible with my military duties. Just before a battle at Borbetomagus, in one of the Gallic provinces, I decided that I could not fight. 'I am a soldier of Christ, I cannot fight,' I told my superiors. Well, I was charged with cowardice and jailed. So, I volunteered to go unarmed to the front of the troops. My superiors were going to let me, but before I could, the enemy vied for peace and the battle never occurred. Then I was released from military service. It was then that I decided I would go into the ministry and I made my way to the city of Tours."

"While in Tours, I became a disciple of Hilary of Poitiers,"

Martin went on. "I went to Illyricum for a while and took sides against the Arians with so much zeal that I was publicly scourged and forced to leave. The bishop of Milan, Auxentius, was an Arian, and he expelled me from the city. I sought shelter on an island called Gallinaria for a while."

"When did you become bishop, uncle?" Patrick asked.

"I became bishop in 371. And I did everything I could do to not become bishop. But the city wanted me. I was so unwilling that I hid in a barn full of geese, but their cackling at my intrusion gave me away! But once I was bishop, I enthusiastically ordered the destruction of pagan temples, altars and sculptures."

After spending two weeks in Tours, Patrick knew it was time to go home. He had enjoyed his time in Tours and was grateful for the opportunity to rest and gain his strength back before travelling the final stretch home.

"Uncle, thank you for taking me in. I can't thank you enough, but I need to go home now," Patrick said over breakfast.

"I guess I can't keep you forever," Martin winked at Patrick. "You do need to go to your parents. I will take you to a captain who will give you passage. We will leave tomorrow."

"I will miss you, Uncle," Patrick said fondly to Martin.

"I will miss you, Patrick. I will be praying for you. God has great things in store for you."

Patrick met Vincentius after his afternoon lecture. "I'm leaving for Britain tomorrow."

"Please, come and visit me in Lerins. You could study there. You would be more than welcome."

After hugging Patrick, Vincentius watched him turn and walk down the long corridor. "I know that young man is going to be mightily used by God one day," he thought.

Martin took Patrick early the next morning to the port to meet the captain who would take Patrick back to Britain.

"Good - bye, Uncle," Patrick said, giving his uncle a warm embrace.

Patrick waved to his uncle as the boat sailed away from the dock. The city of Tours faded into the distance as the boat carrying Patrick sailed for Britain.

Chapter 26

Back Home

Memories came flooding back to Patrick as he once again found himself walking the familiar road toward his family villa. Uncle Martin had sent word to his parents that he was alive and well. Images of his grandfather, Flavius, Maxi, and life as a boy pelted his mind. He thought over and over about what he would say to his parents when he first saw them.

At the sight of the villa Patrick burst into tears. He paid no attention to the servants at their work. Then hearing a familiar bark, Patrick wiped his eyes. Before he knew it he was tackled to the ground by a huge hound dog.

"Maxi!" Patrick roared with delight. The dog sniffed and licked Patrick so much he found it hard to get up. Patrick grabbed Maxi around the neck, holding the dog close. And with Maxi at his side, the two trotted happily toward the villa.

"There's my boy!" Calpurnius shouted, running out from the courtyard. "You are so big and strong now," Calpurnius exclaimed, grabbing Patrick in a bear hug. "You are a man now." He then took Patrick's hands in his own. "These are not the hands of a Roman nobleman. No matter, that will soon change. No more hard work for you, my son. Now come in and find your mother."

Patrick found his mother lying on a couch in the family room. She rose to embrace him and fell into his arms. Patrick was surprised how light and frail she felt.

"Oh, Succat! You will never be taken away from us again, I promise!" Conchessa sobbed as she clung to her son. Calpurnius joined them in the embrace. As servants brought food and refreshments in, Patrick recounted all that had happened to him, of his kidnapping, being a slave, and his escape. Not taking their eyes off him, his parents clung to every word he spoke.

"Now you must go up and get some rest," Conchessa ordered. Patrick didn't argue and gave his mother and father one more hug and turned to go to his room.

As Patrick looked around his old room he found it just the way he had left it. Everything was just as he remembered, as if he had never left. He picked up a sheep bone that was sitting on the stand beside his bed. He remembered carving the hunting dog on it, long ago, when he had been mad at his mother and grandfather. Beside the bone lay the satchel where he kept the knucklebones game Flavius had given him. "So many memories," Patrick thought. "I wonder where Flavius is now and what has become of him?" He opened up the satchel and found the game still inside. Rolling the pieces around in his hand, he remembered playing it with Lupita, and how his grandfather did not like him having the game. It felt strange being back home without Lupita being there. He sat down on his bed and remembered how she would often come into his room and talk with him. "I am never going to take one step outside this villa again!" Patrick promised himself. He let himself sink down into his bed and fell fast asleep.

Patrick woke up and ventured downstairs and found his mother again. He couldn't wait to tell her about his conversion. Servants kept trying to catch quick glimpses at Patrick as they went about their chores, chatting quietly to one another, curious about their master's son who had returned from the life of a slave.

"Mother, I have some very important news to share with you," Patrick began.

Conchessa motioned for her son to sit beside her. "I'm sure you have so much to tell, Patrick. I am eager to hear."

Starting slowly, trying to contain his excitement, Patrick began recounting how the Lord had drawn him to the clearing in the wood, and how he had met the Christian slaves who would gather there for worship. He told her of Killian. Conchessa couldn't hold back tears when Patrick shared how the Scripture he learned as a child came back to him in his time of need.

"I am so thankful to you and to grandfather, mother, for filling my mind with God's word. God certainly used it to bring me to himself."

"Patrick, this means more to me than anything!" She threw her arms around her son. "You are home and hearing of your salvation has brought peace to my soul!"

"I am so happy to be home, mother," Patrick smiled. "So happy to be with you and father again."

The next few days were like a dream to Patrick. He spent his days sitting with his mother, telling her stories of Ireland. He went hunting with his father. Maxi had turned into a brilliant hunting dog. Patrick was very proud of him.

Patrick woke early every morning and climbed the hill outside the villa to pray. He couldn't thank God enough for bringing him home. He marvelled at everything that God had allowed to happen to him and still wondered what God had in store for him.

Chapter 27

A Hard Heart

Patrick and Calpurnius trotted along the wooded path on horseback. Maxi bounced happily along the side of Patrick's horse, sniffing and wagging his tail. Patrick had been praying for the right opportunity to speak to his father about his conversion and his love for his Savior. "Why is it so hard to speak to my father?" he wondered. It frustrated him that he found it so hard to talk of the Lord with his father, after all he had been through in Ireland, dealing with Odhrain and Bain, and even Aelric and Berach.

Sensing the mood was right, Patrick cleared his throat and began, "Father, there is something very important I want to talk with you about."

"What's that, son?" Calpurnius asked, his interest piqued.

"I need to tell you of the most important thing that happened to me in Ireland," Patrick said cautiously.

"You are a man now, my son. I am very proud of you to have survived the horrors of that forsaken place. I can see that your experience there has made you strong and brave," Calpurnius commented.

"Father, it is true that I came through many horrific trials,"

Patrick began. "But God brought me through them. It was God that gave me the strength and courage to survive."

"That's nice, son."

"You see, Father, God changed me when I was in Ireland. He gave me new life." As Patrick talked, he felt the Holy Spirit give him the words.

"Don't tell me you found God in Ireland, Patrick. There is nothing good that can come out of that barbaric world!"

"God found me, Father. Believe me, I wasn't looking for him. I didn't believe in him. I was angry at God for everything that had happened. But I believe God used all those horrible things to bring me to himself, to show me that I am utterly lost without him." Patrick could see his father's face getting hard, but he went on. "God changed my heart. My heart was so full of sin, but Jesus Christ saved me and gave me a heart full of love. I have peace, Father. I want you to know that same love and peace that I have."

Calpurnius looked at his son in cold disbelief. "I never thought I would ever hear you talk like that, Patrick. I will never believe in a God who would allow my son to be taken away from me to live as a slave."

Father and son rode on in silence. Patrick's mind was racing, wondering what he should say next, or if he should say anything at all. He could tell his father was deep in thought. "Please, Lord," Patrick prayed, "show me what to do."

When they got back to the stables, Calpurnius said, "Patrick, you have been through a lot. No father would wish for his son to go through what you have been through. If believing in God helped get you through the past six years, I am grateful, for you are back with me now. But now you are home. You will have no need of God in your life here."

Patrick watched his father hand the reins over to a servant and walk out of the stable. He never realized until now how hard his father really was. He felt a deep sorrow flood over him. Life back home wasn't going to be as easy as he thought.

"Come, Patrick," Calpurnius called. "We need to get ready for the feast."

Chapter 28

The Feast

The villa was bustling with activity when Patrick and Calpurnius returned. Calpurnius had organized a feast for that evening to celebrate Patrick's homecoming. All his father's friends and fellow decurions would be there with their wives. Anyone who was important in Bannavem would be at this feast.

Patrick ran his hand along the fresh, white fabric of his new toga. There was a time, which seemed like so long ago now, when Patrick looked forward to the feasts his father would host. But he wasn't looking forward to this one. With his faith in God he dreaded having to partake in all the revelry. These parties were nothing but wasteful overindulging, drinking, and boasting. After the simple, crude life of a slave, Patrick still felt uncomfortable with the lavish living his father enjoyed.

Patrick could hear the din coming from the dining room as his father's guests talked and laughed. "Oh, Lord, give me grace," he prayed as he approached the room, and taking a deep breath, he stepped through the entrance.

"Friends," Calpurnius burst out at the sight of his son, "rise and toast my son who has returned!" Calpurnius's face was beaming with pride.

All the men and women rose from their seats and lifted their goblets. Holding them high, they all chanted in unison, "To Patrick!"

Patrick lifted his goblet to his lips and sipped the cool wine. All eyes were on him. He recognized most of them, though they were older. The table, as usual, was crowded with overflowing dishes of various meats, fish, bread, cheese, eggs, and vegetables. Patrick made his way to the head of the table and took his seat beside his father.

"Patrick, tell our friends here all about your escape from that brutal Irish ruffian!" Calpurnius boasted.

"Well," Patrick began cautiously. "By the grace of God, I was given the strength to flee. The Lord showed me the way to go. You see, I couldn't have done it without the help of my heavenly Father. Not only did the Lord provide a way of escape for me, he also saved my soul."

The guests started to look uneasy. "Yes, that's all very nice," Calpurnius butted in. "My son is still very tired and weary from his travels. He has been through a lot these last years. Let the feasting begin!" Calpurnius roared as he gave Patrick a rebuking glare.

After all the guests had left, Calpurnius pulled Patrick aside. "What was all that, going on about the Lord saving your soul? You sound like your grandfather. I told you, you have no need of God now!"

Late that night Patrick lay in his bed praying. "Father, please give me the strength to be faithful to you. Give me your courage to stand firm in my faith. Help me to be a good witness to my father. Please open his heart to your gospel. Soften him. Use me, Lord, to lead him to the Savior."

Chapter 29

Church

The next morning was Sunday and Patrick woke feeling hopeful and full of renewed energy. It was the Lord's Day, and he was eager to worship his loving heavenly Father.

"Mother," Patrick said, "I am going to take you to church this morning." Conchessa hadn't been able to go to church in some time because Calpurnius would not go with her.

Hearing his son's voice, Calpurnius stepped into the room. "My son, I have arranged for a hunt today. I could use your help preparing for it."

"Mother hasn't been to church in a long time," Patrick said, challenging his father. "I promised her I would take her. Why don't you come with us?"

Calpurnius gave Patrick a look that showed his disapproval. "Hurry home, son," Calpurnius answered, glaring at Patrick. "There is a lot to do today."

Patrick hardly noticed the hustle and bustle of Bannavem as he rode beside his mother on the cart. He watched with sadness as they passed the baths where he went so often with his grandfather. The servant steered the horse and cart through the marketplace, the basilica, his old school, and the abandoned army barracks. These places were so much a part of his life once. Now he felt like he was passing through a shadow of the distant past. "Was it always like this for a Christian, living in two different worlds?" This town had had such a hold on him when he was a boy. Now, when he passed through the town and looked into people's eyes, he saw emptiness and troubled souls. He saw people striving for the things of this earth, for power, wealth, and pleasure.

"Patrick, you're deep in thought," Conchessa said to her son. "We are here."

The servant helped Conchessa down from the cart. Patrick jumped down and took his mother's arm. "I'm so happy to be going to church today, Patrick. I'm especially glad to be going with you," his mother said, giving her son's arm a squeeze.

"I'm very happy, too, Mother, to be able to take you to church and worship with you. I wish Father would come. I'm sorry he has not taken you."

Mother and son walked into the little stone church and found a seat on a wooden bench along the right side. Patrick could still see his grandfather, as clear as ever, standing at the front.

After the church service, Patrick and his mother stayed behind as the other worshippers filed out of the stone building. It was so small compared to his Uncle Martin's church. He remembered how he would sit bored out of his mind, fidgeting during the whole service. He remembered his grandfather glaring at him sternly, trying to subdue him into listening.

"Patrick!" called the priest, laying a hand on Patrick's shoulder. Hearing his name jolted him from his memories.

"It is good to see you, Patrick," the priest said. "I knew your grandfather well. And I remember you when you were a boy," he added, smiling.

"Thank you for the service," said Patrick a little embarrassed. He felt ashamed of his attitude and behavior as a child.

"Your grandfather would be so proud of you." Hearing the priest say this filled Patrick's heart with such joy. "He is proud of you," the priest added. These words coming from another man of God gave Patrick such an assurance and swept away any shame and guilt he had for not heeding his grandfather's counsel.

Back at the villa, the servant dropped Patrick and Conchessa off in the courtyard and then drove to the stables to unhitch the horse. A soft drizzle of rain welcomed them as they made their way to the house. Patrick noticed two servants entering the courtyard, pulling a cart laden with wine barrels. He wasted no time in hurrying over to help the men lift the barrels off the cart. The surprised servants gaped at Patrick and thanked him.

"What do you think you're doing?" Calpurnius roared as he stepped out from the house. Patrick whirled around, shocked at his father's loud inquisition.

"They were having difficulty," Patrick protested. "I didn't want them to drop the barrels. And besides, they could hurt their backs."

"You are not a slave, Patrick! You are my son! You will not do a slave's work!" Calpurnius bellowed and stormed off.

Patrick helped his mother inside, then went out again, and climbed to the top of the hill where he would often go to think when he was a boy. He stared out across the sea and over toward where Ireland lay. When he was a slave in Ireland Patrick would often climb to the top of Slemish and look out toward Britain, longing to be home.

It was strange being home. Patrick mouthed the word "home" silently to himself as he stared out toward the sea. Strangely, it didn't feel like home anymore. The villa wasn't the same. His parents weren't the same. He wasn't the same. After longing so much to be back in Britain again, Patrick felt discontent. He felt he didn't belong here anymore. He couldn't help thinking that God had something more for him than just taking over management of his father's villa. After all he had been through—being kidnapped, working as a slave, and being born again—he couldn't help wondering why God would take him through all that just to run a villa.

Patrick found himself drawn to Bannavem in a different way now. He enjoyed worship in the little church, and he also enjoyed talking with the priest, Father Albon. Father Albon had talked with Patrick about becoming more involved in the services and ministries. He had even mentioned to Patrick that he could perhaps follow in his grandfather's footsteps one day and become a priest. The thought of that inspired Patrick and gave him a hope, a purpose here in Bannavem. Maybe this was God's calling on his life, he began to wonder.

The hot sun beamed down on the servants as they raked hay. They waved at Patrick as he walked along the path leading from Bannavem to the villa. Patrick waved back to them as he hummed his favorite hymn.

Patrick was in high spirits. He had just come from the church in town where he had helped Father Albon administer some bread to the poor. Calpurnius met him in the courtyard.

"Patrick, you are spending too much time with that priest," Calpurnius scolded. "I want you to start taking on some of the responsibilities here at the villa." Patrick knew this was coming. He knew his father wasn't happy with him going to worship every Sunday. Now he was going to have to tell his father his dreams of becoming a priest! Patrick shuddered at the thought.

His mother was overjoyed at the idea of Patrick taking after his grandfather. She encouraged him in everything Father Albon wanted him to do. "Mother was thrilled to hear of my conversion," he thought silently. "I know Father is overjoyed to have me back. He shows it in his own way, I know. But Father is so hopeful of handing down the villa to me. The truth is, I enjoy the duties of the church more than I do the villa. And I enjoy spending time with Father Albon more than I do my own father."

Chapter 30

The Voice of the Irish

P atrick lay in bed that night deep in thought. His head was swimming. He felt constrained, like a bird in a cage anxious to be free. "Funny," he thought to himself, "I couldn't wait to be free from Ireland, and now that I am, I feel more imprisoned than ever!"

Killian and the group he used to worship with in the Wood of Fochlad kept coming to his mind. "How were they getting on?" he wondered. He thought of how he had wanted to write down scriptures for the little group to be used in worship. Patrick was concerned for their safety, wondering if any harm had come to them because of his escape. He knew God had planned for him to leave Ireland, but he still felt guilty and responsible for the little group.

Patrick also thought a lot about Aelric and Berach. Would he see these men in heaven? He prayed every day for their salvation, just as he prayed for his father. They were in God's hands which was the best place for them.

And Lupita also still haunted his thoughts. Was she still alive? Was she still in Ireland? Would he ever see her again on this earth?

All these thoughts were swirling around in Patrick's mind. He tried to relax and focus on praying with the Lord. With so many heavy burdens, he knew the best thing to do was to take them before his Lord and lay them at his feet. After a while Patrick was so deep in communion with his heavenly Father that he was unconscious of the world around him. The Holy Spirit was filling his heart with comfort and peace and security as he felt transported to a heavenly place.

While abiding in the Lord's presence he caught a glimpse of a man coming to him with his arms full of letters. The man stared right at Patrick with imploring eyes. "My name is Victorius," the man said in an Irish accent. Victorius reached out his hand and gave one of the letters to Patrick. On the letter was the heading, "The Voice of the Irish." As Patrick began to read the letter, he imagined he could hear the voices of the church that met in the wood of Fochlad. Over and over he heard their cries, "We appeal to you, holy boy, to come and walk among us." The cries pierced Patrick's heart.

Patrick woke the next morning with a start. He knew at that very instant he was destined to go back to Ireland. God had answered his prayers in a clear and marvelous way. He felt no more doubt and confusion as to what God intended for his life.

"Oh, thank you, Father," Patrick prayed. "Thank you for unfolding to me your plan for my life, and for using me to bring your salvation to the Irish."

All day Patrick couldn't get the vision out of his mind. How would he get back to Ireland? The reality of what God wanted him to do was so clear. Just as God had come through on his promise to help him escape from Ireland, Patrick was confident that God would provide a way for him to go back.

Chapter 31

Obeying God's Call

Everything that had happened to Patrick made so much sense now. God had used his captivity to bring him to a saving knowledge of Christ. And God had used his captivity to shape him into the very man he needed to take the gospel back to the Irish!

Patrick spent much time in prayer and fasting concerning his call to the Irish. His heart was filled with exuberance at the thought of being used to show the love of Christ. His Lord who had laid down his life for him would now speak through him!

With this new revelation and divine assurance, Patrick now had the confidence to confront his father. He found him in the librarium, going over some documents.

Patrick had been rehearsing this moment over and over in his mind. After all that he had been through, being kidnapped, seeing his grandfather die right before his eyes, being torn away from his parents, watching Lupita vanish, working as a slave, suffering abuse from Gosact and Odhrain, and more, this was perhaps the hardest thing the Lord would have him undertake. How was he going to tell his father that the Lord was calling him to go back to the people who had taken him away from him?

"But, Patrick, how can you even think of going back there?" Calpurnius thundered. "After all they have done to you! They kidnapped you, stripped you of everything! They turned you into a slave and brutally treated you! You will not go back! I will hear no more of this madness!" Calpurnius slammed his fist down on the table and stormed out of the librarium.

"Oh, Lord," Patrick prayed. "Please help my father to understand. Open his eyes. Open his heart to the gospel. Then he will know why I have to go back."

Patrick found his father in the stables. "Father, please listen to me. Let me explain."

"How could you do this to us? How could you do this to your mother? This sort of talk will just ruin her. She about died of a heartache when you were taken away," Calpurnius stormed on. "She is just about hanging on to life now. She could not bear to have you leave us again."

Calpurnius took the reins from the servant's hands and mounted his horse. "Patrick, you get this madness out of your head!" Striking the horse hard, making it bolt from the stall and out of the stables, Calpurnius left Patrick and the servant in the dust.

Patrick found his mother crying in the living room. He put his arm around her and tried to comfort her. "You see, Mother," Patrick began. "My life has a whole new meaning now. I know for sure this is God's plan for me."

"But the people here need the Lord, too," Conchessa sobbed. "You could become a priest here, like your grandfather. Then you could stay here. And you could still help with the villa."

Patrick hated seeing his mother like this. It hurt him knowing that once again he was the cause of so much pain for her.

"The Irish have no one, Mother. They need someone to bring the gospel to them. I am certain this is what God has been molding me for. Everything that I endured during my captivity was God's way of preparing me to take the gospel to the Irish." As Conchessa listened to her son, uncontrollable tears flowed down her cheeks.

"Mother, I know you desire people to come to know Christ. Even the Irish are God's children. God showed me his love when I didn't deserve it. And now God wants to use me to show his love to the Irish. Can't you see that everything that has happened in my life has led up to this? I know that God had me captured and made me work as a slave because I had to be humbled. I had to be brought to nothing. And now I know that he had me live and work in Ireland for six years, immersed in their culture, so that I would get to know them. I can think, feel, share, and suffer the way the Irish do. God had to rid me of all identification with my own culture. It has been so hard settling back into life in Britain, Mother. You know that. My life has totally changed, and I cannot escape that. The reason for that change is made clear now."

The sound of a horse galloping into the courtyard came in the open window. "Your father is home again," Conchessa said anxiously.

Patrick stood and braced himself as his father stormed into the living room.

"If you endeavor to go through with this mission of yours, then you will give up your title forever. You will be stripped of every ounce of superiority of your Roman status. You will no longer be a son of mine!" Calpurnius roared.

"Father, please," Patrick cried with desperation.

Calpurnius glared at his son with eyes full of rage. Patrick had witnessed his father losing his temper many times but had never experienced his wrath directed solely at himself. Clutching his mother's hand, with his heart pounding in his chest, Patrick stood firm and looked straight into his father's angry eyes.

"My mind is made up," Patrick calmly stated to his father, his face firm and unflinching. With determination in his eyes Patrick held his composure until his father exited the living room.

With his father out of the room, Patrick slumped to the sofa, his mind dizzy with what had happened. He felt exhausted from his emotions waging war within himself. In an ironic sort of way Patrick felt good having stood up to his father like that. To be able to speak his mind to his father had confirmed even more to Patrick that he was doing the right thing. "Oh Lord, thank you for giving me strength," he prayed to himself.

"Patrick, please, your father will come around. He just needs time," his mother pleaded, sitting down next to him. Patrick did feel torn about leaving his family again, especially his mother. But the call of the Irish was pulling him.

"Mother, you know I can't turn away from God's calling." He looked imploringly into his mother's eyes.

"Where will you go?" Conchessa asked with tears choking her voice.

"I will make my way back to Uncle Martin, and then I think onto Lerins. There is a monastery there where I can study. My friend Vincentius said I am welcome there. I will send word when I can."

Patrick let go of his mother's hand and made his way to his room. He knew that now was the time to go. If he stayed any longer things would just get worse between his father and him. Patrick quickly stuffed what he would need into a large cloth bag and slung it over his shoulder.

When he made his way to the front door, Patrick gave his mother one last embrace. "Mother, I love you. I will be praying for you." He stooped down to give Maxi one last pat on the head. "You look after Mother, Maxi." Finding it hard not to linger, he turned and walked out through the courtyard. Glancing back, he saw his father standing in the doorway with his arm around his mother, watching him. Patrick was leaving his family, the villa, his position, and everything of this world behind to follow Christ.

Patrick stopped by the church in Bannavem to say goodbye to Father Albon.

"You have become very dear to me, Patrick," Father Albon said. "I will miss you."

"I will miss you, too, Father Albon," Patrick replied. "I have learned so much from you. Thank you for your support and guidance."

"Before you go, Patrick, I want to share something with you. I believe you are like the prophet Elijah. Elijah was used by God to influence kings. I believe God has destined to use you for great things, Patrick. But Elijah was also a lonely and unpopular prophet who had to say unpopular things to people in power. God spoke to Elijah in a still, small voice. Always listen to God, Patrick. He is going to use you mightily."

Father Albon had spoken to Patrick so movingly that Patrick felt himself close to tears. "Thank you, Father, I don't know what to say." Patrick paused and then added, "Your words have given me assurance of my call. Thank you."

"Remember that when you go to Ireland it will not be you speaking. It will be the Spirit of God speaking through you. He who gave his life for you, it is he who speaks in you. God has spoken and now you must obey."

Patrick left Father Albon and headed to the port of Bannavem. He paid passage on a ship sailing for Tours. Boarding the boat, Patrick gave one last glance at Bannavem. "God has called, and I must obey."

Chapter 32

Training

I t was good to see Uncle Martin again. Martin was surprised to see him, but excited about Patrick's mission. "I knew God chose you for something very special," Martin told Patrick. "You will have to study hard to become a bishop."

"I know I lack in my academic learning, Uncle," Patrick said. "My schooling was interrupted when I was kidnapped."

"The church has never undertaken a mission like this before, Patrick." Martin's tone became more serious. "It might not be as easy as you think to get the support you need."

"I know God will show me the way to go," Patrick added confidently. "He always has, and I'm sure he won't let me down this time."

"Vincentius will be a good teacher," Martin assured Patrick. "Lerins will be a good place for you to study. Remember that Christ is strong in your weakness. You have the grace of God in your life. He called you to this task and he will enable you to carry it out."

After staying with his uncle for a few more days, Patrick made his final preparations to travel to Lerins. Martin sent word to Conchessa telling her that Patrick had arrived safely and was on his way to Lerins. He was eager to begin his studies. Lerins was one step closer to Ireland!

Patrick was twenty- three now. The thought of studying again was a little daunting to him. He was also self-conscious of the fact that his education had been interrupted and was lacking. He wondered if the brothers at Lerins would accept him.

Trying not to dwell on his worries, instead Patrick focused on Christ. It was Christ who called him to this mission, so he was convinced he would succeed. He would just have to wait and rely on the Lord to show him how it was all going to unfold.

Patrick thanked the captain and stepped onto the shore of the island of Lerinus. The crew of the boat then began to make ready for the half mile sail back to mainland Gaul. Patrick was very excited to see Vincentius again. He was also looking forward to spending some extended periods of uninterrupted devotion with the Lord.

Lerinus was the second largest island in the Lerins. The monastery was founded by Honoratus, who cultivated the island and made it a place where men could go to get away from the strife and turmoil of life. It attracted men who wanted a place of solace and refuge where they could spend long periods of time in prayer and devotion to God.

Patrick breathed in the smell of the allepo pines and eucalyptus trees along the shore. The air was full of their scent mixed with the salty sea. He found a path that wound its way through the trees. Black snakes slithered quickly across the path to avoid being trampled on by the large intruder.

The end of the path took Patrick to a clearing with some crude huts scattered around. Patrick walked up to the biggest looking one and opened the door. Kneeling on a woolen mat on the floor was a man with a familiar face.

Patrick could hardly contain his excitement. "Um, excuse me," he said, trying to sound solemn.

Vincentius looked up, startled, and gasped, "Patrick!" He ran over to Patrick and embraced him in a big hug. "Your uncle sent word that you were coming, but it's still a pleasant surprise to have you here," Vincentius said with a beaming smile.

"It is good to see you," Patrick said. "I'm sorry to interrupt your prayers."

"I was actually praying for you. You are very welcome here, Patrick. You can stay as long as you like. I will have word sent to Bishop Martin so that he knows you have arrived safely."

"Thank you, Vincentius," Patrick replied. "That will be most appreciated. My uncle will then send word to my mother."

"Good. Then, come, Patrick. You must have something to eat. When I met you on the way to Tours I could tell that God had you marked out for something great. I want to hear how Lerins can help you in your calling."

The two men passed a stone well where a man was gathering water in a bucket tied to the end of a rope. "Would you like a drink?" the man asked, holding a tin cup out to Patrick.

Patrick sipped the cool, refreshing water, letting it slide down his parched throat. "Thank you," he told the man gratefully.

"The water here is sweet which flows in the midst of the bitterness of the sea," replied the man in a soft, peaceful voice.

"Lupus, this is Patrick. He has come here to study," Vincentius said.

Lupus reached out his hand and shook Patrick's. "Welcome, Patrick," he said with a grin. "I hope you find Lerins a haven in the midst of the stormy sea."

Vincentius guided Patrick toward a cluster of huts. After dumping his bag into one of them, the two men walked past small fields separated by low stone walls. Sheep were grazing in one of the fields. Crops were growing in another. Grape vines made long green rows in another.

Ahead of them now was a wooden structure sitting atop a short hill. There was a stone path leading up to the building. "This is used as our meeting place," Vincentius explained. "We have worship here, as well as lectures."

Patrick followed Vincentius up the stony path. Just to the left of the front door was a stone column. "That is a Constantinian milestone," Vincentius said. "Honoratus found it here on the island."

From the top of the hill Patrick could see over the tree - tops and out toward the sea. He saw a larger island further out in the distance.

"That is the island of Lero," Vincentius said. "One of our brothers, Eucherius, lives there. After his wife Galla died he built a hut there. He has written a treatise in praise of the hermit's life."

"Interesting," thought Patrick.

"There is also a Roman port and baths on Lero. The port is used as part of a maritime route between Rome and Spain," Vincentius explained.

Walking through the door, a huge, open room greeted Patrick. Light shone in from large windows lining the walls. Patrick's feet made scuffing sounds on the dirt floor as he and Vincentius made their way over to the left side of the room. Vincentius sat down at a small wooden table and motioned for Patrick to do the same.

"Now, my friend," Vincentius began, propping his elbows on the table and holding his chin in his hands. "Tell me all about your call to go to Ireland and preach the gospel."

Never tiring of an opportunity to share about how the Lord was working in his life, Patrick began to tell Vincentius everything. He explained in great detail about his calling, his parents, and especially how the Holy Spirit was drawing him to go to Ireland.

It was good for Patrick to express his fears and concerns about his lack of education and feeling of unworthiness to Vincentius. Particularly on Patrick's mind was the objection some of the bishops had made against him going to Ireland to evangelize and share the gospel. They had no concern for the lost. Their only concern was for power and that Ireland have a bishop. Patrick was very aware that his focus was not the same as the other church leaders and he felt very alone.

Vincentius assured Patrick that the Lord Almighty, who had called him to this task, would be with him every step of the way. "God will equip you and strengthen you," Vincentius encouraged Patrick. "You will have the Lord always at your side."

As the two old friends continued to talk, Lupus brought in two plates of food and set them down on the table. Vincentius lit a small candle and the light outside began to fade as the darkness came in to take its turn covering the earth.

The years Patrick spent at Lerins had a great influence on him and had been very good for his soul. He studied hard and acquired an excellent knowledge of the Scriptures and a solid grounding in teaching. He loved being able to spend days in prayer, fasting, and studying the Word of God. This was necessary for Patrick, laying a good foundation for his future. But he felt it was time to take a further step toward his mission.

"I think it is time for me to move on, Vincentius," Patrick told his friend. "I think the time has come for me to put into practice what I have learned. My time here has been of great benefit to me, and I will always be grateful."

With Vincentius's blessing, Patrick made his way to Auxerre, situated on the River Yonne in central Gaul. The year was now 412 and Patrick was 25 years old. While at Auxerre he spent fifteen additional years in rigorous training under Germanus. His time at Lerins had been one of quiet and reflective study, where his time at Auxerre was of a more practical nature. Patrick loved the missionary work he accompanied Germanus on. It gave him a taste and whetted his appetite for spreading the gospel in Ireland.

Patrick sealed the letter he had written to his mother and blew out the candle on the table. He lay on his bed in the darkness, thinking about all that had happened that day. Germanus had burst into Patrick's room late in the morning with the news that Palladius, a fellow student of Patrick's, had died. Patrick's emotions were now at war inside of him. He felt deep sadness at his friend's death but also excitement for what could be in store for himself.

It had been a huge blow to Patrick when Palladius had been selected to go to Ireland. He spent many nights wrestling with God in prayer, wondering why, after all the Lord had brought him through and knowing his passionate devotion for the Irish, he would send someone else to Ireland. Germanus had fought hard to persuade Pope Celestine that Patrick should be the one to go to Ireland, but in the end, Palladius had been chosen.

"All that needs to happen now for me to go to Ireland is for me to become a bishop," he thought. Patrick knew that the Pope was more concerned about establishing and confirming an ecclesiastical presence in Ireland among the Irish believers and was not interested in the conversion of the pagan Irish. The Pope did not share Patrick's burning zeal for evangelizing the lost and did not consider converting pagans as a qualification for becoming a bishop.

Many of the other priests thought Patrick was crazy. They tried in vain to discourage him from desiring to go to Ireland to convert the lost. Patrick could hear them whispering behind his back. "Imagine him going off to try and convert the people who captured him! A ministry like that is doomed to fail." Patrick was all too aware that the evil one was trying his hardest to tempt him to doubt his calling.

And now, Patrick could hardly believe this moment had come. A council of bishops had chosen Patrick to take Palladius's place, and Patrick was now a consecrated bishop! Some on the council thought his mission was too rash and dangerous and feared for his safety, especially after Palladius's death. Others thought he was unqualified.

Despite all his limitations, Patrick was sure of his calling and had complete trust in God his Father, a trust he had learned on the mountain. "I am willing to die for the Irish, so that they can know and believe the gospel!" Patrick had triumphantly persuaded the council. Patrick was prepared to suffer and die to bring the light of Christ to the dark Irish. "It's precious souls that Jesus wants. Jesus paid for the sins of the lost Irish with his life! And God has called me to tell the Irish that Jesus loves them and died for them!"

"Patrick, you will be the first missionary bishop," said Germanus fondly. "May God use you to bring the gospel to many still in darkness."

The year 432 would turn out to be a year that would change the island of Ireland forever—and even the world!

Chapter 33

Dichu

Patrick and his companions rowed into view of the Irish shore. The coastline seemed to be drawing him, pulling him. "Come to us," the voice of his dream kept penetrating his mind. It was as if the island was speaking to him. His heart full of anticipation and his body full of nervous energy, Patrick could hardly contain the emotions that swept through him. How different this trip had been from the first one which had brought him here. He had first come in chains against his will, a proud and defiant teenager. Now he came freely, a humble man who desired to serve the Lord.

Once on shore, the group unloaded their supplies and hid them in the brush. Patrick hugged his Latin Bible tightly to his chest. He was finally back on Irish soil. With every step he took he could feel the Holy Spirit giving him strength, pulling him, spurring him on to preach the gospel. The voice of Victorious kept ringing in his head. He would not be content and at peace until he had preached to the Irish. His two companions, Fith and Auxillius, followed him from behind. They walked a short distance inward from the shore and found a place to rest. There were low hills covering the land and a herd of swine was dozing in a mud pasture nearby.

"Oh, Father, thank you for bringing us here safely," Patrick led the others in prayer as his companions bowed their heads. "Be with us and guide us as we embark on our mission. Thank you for using us to speak your gospel to the Irish. Our Father, we pray that every tongue here will confess that Jesus Christ is Lord and God. May your Holy Spirit make them believe in your Son. We confess and adore you, the one Triune God. Give us courage and perseverance and keep our focus on Christ. Speak your words from our mouths. Amen."

"Amen," Fith and Auxillius responded.

"How are we ever going to evangelize this island?" Auxillius asked.

"We aren't," Patrick assured. "God is!" He smiled back at his two friends. Fith and Auxillius were very loyal friends. They had stuck by him when others had laughed at his idea of being a missionary to Ireland.

"We are mere instruments in God's hands," Patrick went on to explain. "We are clay in the hands of the Potter. God will use us and work through us to bring his salvation to the Irish. Do you believe that, Auxillius?" Patrick asked.

"Yes, Patrick. I just wish I had your great faith."

Patrick loved Fith and Auxillius. He was very grateful of their companionship. The three had grown close like brothers as Patrick discipled them.

"Remember, brothers," Patrick said, taking on a more serious tone, "we have no protection under the law here. Your Roman status will do you no good. Have courage and faith."

The little band of missionaries did not realize that they were being watched. A swineherd saw the strangers from his hut. He had watched the trio sail up along the shore and land. He made his way as fast as he could to his master Dichu's house, which stood atop the highest hill.

"Master!" the servant yelled, storming into the house. "Bandits are here. I saw them. They are hiding not far from the shore, near the swine."

Dichu grabbed his sword. "How many of them are there?" he asked.

"Only three," the servant replied in a worried voice.

"Come!" Dichu ordered his servant. "Do you have your staff? Good, we can take them." The two of them bounded out the door.

Dichu followed his servant as they crept stealthily through the fields, past the snorting and grunting pigs. The servant held up his arm and motioned for Dichu to halt. He pointed to where Patrick, Fith, and Auxillius were hiding. They could hear the men talking.

Drawing their weapons, Dichu and the servant charged the little group. They came crashing through the brush, terrifying the startled missionaries. Dichu, reaching the group first, swung his sword, aiming to strike at Fith.

Just at that same instant Patrick stood up, overcome with courage from the Holy Spirit, and grabbed Dichu's attacking arm. He held his arm in such a tight grip that Dichu dropped his sword. The swineherd, seeing his master in Patrick's submission, let go of Auxillius and went to rescue Dichu.

"We mean you no harm," Patrick exclaimed. "We come in peace, the true peace of the living Son of God." Patrick let go of Dichu. Overcome by Patrick's meekness and authority, the swineherd backed off.

"What do you want with us, then?" Dichu asked.

"We want nothing of you," Patrick responded. "We have something we want to share with you."

There was something about Patrick that piqued Dichu's curiosity. He was strong but gentle. There was love in his eyes. Dichu felt strangely drawn to hear what Patrick had to say.

Sitting in the field, near the pigs, Patrick explained to Dichu and his servant how the one true God created the world and how the world had become full of sin. Master and servant sat captivated, listening to the gospel.

"But God in his rich love and mercy sent his one and only Son, Christ Jesus, into the world, to die in our place to take away our sin," Patrick proclaimed.

The Holy Spirit spoke through Patrick and opened the hearts of the two men to receive the good news. Tears started streaming down their faces when they heard that Jesus gave up his life for them because of his love for them.

"Do you believe you are a sinner?" Patrick asked Dichu and his servant.

"Yes," they replied, choking on their tears.

"Do you believe that only Jesus Christ can save you from your sin?"

"Yes, I believe," spoke Dichu and his servant together. "We want Jesus to take away our sin." It was obvious that they were filled with conviction.

"Do you believe that it is by grace you are saved through faith in the Lord Jesus Christ?" Patrick inquired further.

"We believe with all our hearts."

Patrick knelt beside Dichu and his servant and led them in prayer. The two men bowed their heads and gave their hearts to the Lord.

The small group embraced, and Patrick, Fith, and Auxillius welcomed their two new brothers into the faith. Patrick took the men down to the beach and baptized them. "Dichu, son of Trechim, I baptize you in the name of the Father, the Son, and the Holy Spirit."

Dichu led Patrick, Fith, and Auxillius up to his fortress and showed him a large barn, or sabhall, on a hill next to his house.

"I grant this sabhall to you as a gift, Patrick," Dichu promised out of sincere gratefulness.

"I will dedicate this place to be used as a Christian place of worship," Patrick replied. In the coming days Patrick and his companions, along with their new brothers in Christ, turned the sabhall into a church. Patrick, Fith, and Auxillius taught and instructed Dichu and his household in the faith. Using his chiefly influence over the region, Dichu sent word that everyone in his rath were to come and listen to the gospel of Jesus Christ.

After a service of worship one evening, Patrick spoke to Fith, Auxillius, and Dichu. "The Lord has greatly blessed the planting of this first seed of the gospel in Ireland. I must now go to other areas."

The others listened and nodded in agreement, knowing that the time of moving on was approaching. "My work is done here," Patrick continued. "I believe it is time to hand over the work here and seek my old master, Miliucc."

"Lomman will want to go with you, you know." Dichu nodded over to where a young man with bright red hair was talking excitedly with a group of children. Lomman had been one of the earliest converts of Dichu's rath.

The children dispersed from Lomman, laughing at his funny antics as they went. Dichu called for Lomman to come over and explained that Patrick would be leaving soon to take the gospel to other parts of Ireland.

"I want to go with you," Lomman said to Patrick.

"We would be grateful of your company and help," Patrick said and welcomed Lomman into his band, hugging him. He admired the zeal and passion in this young man, which reminded him so much of himself when he was his age.

"I must find Miliucc," Patrick told his friends. The dream he had back home in which Victorious came to him with the letter entitled, "The Voice of the Irish" had been gnawing at him ever since he set foot in Ireland. He wondered if Odhrain was still alive and in control of his old master. And he wondered if he would have to confront Gosact again.

Chapter 34

A Happy Reunion

Waving goodbye to Dichu and his people, the group of four missionaries sailed their little boat toward Inbher De, near the mouth of the Bray River. The river reached the coast just north of the long ness that runs out into the sea at Wicklow. Patrick marveled at the strange looking ships being rid of their cargo by foreign faces. Inbher De was a chief port for mariners coming from south Britain and Gaul.

"This is where Palladius died," Patrick told his companions. "King Nathi rules here. We must beware."

The group attempted to land on shore, but as they were pulling in their boat, a band of locals came out of the forest's edge. There was anger in their eyes as they stood holding their swords poised for attack. A fierce-looking man with a dislodged tooth stepped forward. "Set foot on our land and we will attack you!" he growled.

Patrick sensed from the Spirit that they were to move on from this place. "We go in peace," he called out. The missionaries hauled their boat back into the water. Not content until they were out of sight, the rough warriors withdrew back into the forest.

One of Patrick's duties as bishop was to visit and confirm the

Christian communities that already existed. Patrick was eager to get to Fochlad where he had worshipped as a slave, to see Killian and the others, where his vision of Victorius kept calling him.

The group made their way to the Skerries off the east coast, north of Dublin. They rested for a few days and spent some time in prayer on a tiny island.

The sea was calm as Patrick and his friends came to the mouth of the River Boyne. A small group of people were scattered on the beach mending their fishing nets. They grabbed their spears that were lying on the ground next to them, ready to defend themselves against the strangers getting out of the boat.

"Do not fear," Patrick called out in Gaelic.

Seeing that the men were unarmed, the cautious group of Irish gathered to inspect the mysterious travellers who spoke their language.

"Where do you come from?" one of the men asked. "You speak our tongue, yet you are not of here."

"We are messengers of the Lord Jesus Christ, the one true God," Patrick exclaimed with excitement.

"Who is this one true God?" one of the fishermen asked, eyeing the travellers suspiciously.

"We will tell you about him," Patrick explained. With great joy Patrick started explaining the gospel. As the assembled group listened, their faces softened as their hearts were being warmed by the Holy Spirit's wooing.

Tears of joy streamed down Patrick's face as seven men were baptized at the mouth of the Boyne. "Thank you, Father, for these precious souls," Patrick prayed.

"Who is your chief, and will you take us to him?" Patrick asked the men.

One of the older men with white hair and an ancient, wrinkled face spoke, "Our chief is Fedilmid, son of King Laoghaire, the high king."

At the mention of King Laoghaire, Patrick's mind jolted back many years to the time when he sat shivering, tied to the post with the ale servant in King Niall's great hall. Laoghaire was Niall's son who now sat on the throne.

"I wish to speak with your chief," Patrick replied, snapping out of his memories.

"It is getting dark," the old man said. "We will spend the night here, then in the morning we will show you the way."

The next morning Patrick, Fith, Auxillius, and Lomman climbed back into their boat and followed the others as they sailed up the Boyne. They landed at the Ford of the Alder, where Trim, the rath of the new converts, was located.

The Irish men helped Fith and Auxillius unload their boat and pull it up onto the shore. Fith and Auxillius were bombarded with questions as the Irish asked about the strange objects in the boat. As the boat was being unloaded, Patrick grabbed some silver and gold coins Pope Celestine had given him for his journey. Patrick knew that gifts were needed to be granted an audience with chiefs and kings.

Standing on the bank of the ford a young boy was watching Lomman picking up a bunch of scrolls. Lomman, with his charisma and fiery red hair, had a way of attracting children.

"What are those?" the dark-haired, fair-skinned boy asked.

Lomman looked up to see the boy staring at the scrolls in his hand. The lad was dressed in finer tunics than the other Irish he had seen so far. "These are the words of God," Lomman said with a smile.

The awe-struck boy slid down the bank and joined Lomman. "Lugh's words are in there?"

Lomman smiled at the simple naivety and childish wonder of the boy. "No, these scrolls contain the words of the living, one true God," Lomman explained.

Hearing the conversation, Patrick came over. There was something very familiar about the boy that puzzled Patrick. "What my friend says is true," Patrick said. "Would you like to hear about the one true God?"

The boy nodded his head enthusiastically. Together, Patrick and Lomman explained the gospel slowly and carefully, starting with who God is and how he created the world, and ending with Jesus' death and resurrection. The boy listened eagerly as Patrick read the words of God from the scrolls.

"You see, God is three persons," Patrick explained as he knelt and plucked a shamrock from the grassy bank. He pointed to the three leaves. "There is God the Father, God the Son, and God the Holy Spirit. They are three persons, but one God. Just like the Shamrock has three leaves but is one Shamrock."

"Fortchernn! Fortchernn!" a woman's voice was heard calling out loudly.

"I know that voice," Patrick realized to himself. He stood up and couldn't believe who he saw making her way down to the river.

"Lupita!" Patrick screamed, running for his long, lost sister.

Brother and sister fell into each other's arms, weeping. "I thought I would never see you again," Lupita said, her eyes moist from crying. "I thought I would never see anyone from Britain again, let alone you!"

"I searched and searched for you, Lupita," Patrick told his sister. "Now God has answered my prayers."

"What are you doing here?" Stepping away from Patrick, Lupita looked at him curiously. "Are you still a slave?" she asked, concerned.

"No, no. I am no longer a slave to an earthly master," Patrick said. "But I am now a slave to Christ. God has called me to bring the gospel to the Irish."

Lupita stared at her brother in total amazement. "Come, Patrick, you must meet my husband, Fedilmid, and tell us your story." Grabbing Fortchernn by the hand, Lupita led Patrick up the bank of the ford, and to the hall of the rath at Trim. Lomman went to find Fith and Auxillius.

Inside, the great hall was very similar to Miliucc's. A man with broad shoulders and long, red hair was standing at a table in the far end of the room, in conversation with a druid.

"Fedilmid," Lupita called out to her husband. "My brother, Patrick, has been found!"

The druid cast an unsettling glare at Patrick.

"Word has reached our lands about a Britain who has arrived on our shores," Fedilmid declared solemnly. "Welcome to Trim. Lupita has told me much about you. You will dine with me tonight and tell me what has happened to you, and why you are here."

As Fedilmid was speaking, the druid eyed Patrick with grave suspicion. Lupita cast the druid a warning look as she led Patrick and her son out of the hall.

"I do not trust that man," the druid confided to Fedilmid. "We must be wary of him. We must heed the prophecy."

"The man is my wife's brother, Mordan," Fedilmid said.

Fedilmid had a feast prepared in honor of Patrick. Patrick gave his testimony of how he and Lupita had been captured by Irish raiders when he was sixteen, and he sold as a slave to Miliucc. He then recounted how the Lord had saved him and provided a way of escape back to Britain. Finally, Patrick told how God had called him to go back to Ireland to tell the Irish people about the one true God, the Lord Jesus Christ, and his salvation for sinners.

"And he has the words of the one true God on a scroll, Father," Fortchernn interrupted.

"Let us hear from these words of your God, then," Fedilmid expressed with interest.

"Sire, I do not think this is wise," Mordan whispered into the king's ear. "You know what the prophecy says."

"Enough, Mordan," Fedilmid slammed his fist down on the table. "I want to hear the words of this God. I will judge for myself if they are true."

Lupita was beside herself with excitement and anticipation as Mordan skulked away from the table and Patrick read from the scriptures.

"I am the way, the truth and the life. No one comes to the Father except through me," Patrick read.

That evening Patrick had the pleasure of leading Fedilmid and his nephew, Fortchernn, to the Lord.

With the son of the high king now a Christian, Patrick was given a strong position in the land. Through Fedilmid's influence and protection, he was now able to reach more Irish people with the gospel.

"Fedilmid," Patrick began. "I must seek my old master Miliucc. His soul weighs heavy on my heart."

"Then you must go," Fedilmid replied. "But beware. Odhrain still has control over chief Miliucc and his son Gosact. You will be out of my protection there."

"With your permission, Lomman would like to remain here with you, to instruct you and teach you in the ways of the Lord."

"Oh, please, Father," Fortchernn pleaded. Fortchernn had grown very fond of Lomman.

"Very well," the king replied. "I want my people to know more about the one true God, and to hear from his words."

Lupita clung to Patrick, imploring him not to go. How many times did he have to say goodbye to loved ones? His heart was torn between his family and his calling. He remembered his mother begging him not to go back to Ireland.

Slowly bringing himself to find the words, Patrick loosened Lupita's grip. "Lupita, my dear sister. I need to obey the Lord. There are more Irish souls who need to hear the gospel." He looked at her with tender affection.

Lupita nodded, tears streaming from her eyes. Patrick boarded his little boat where he joined Fith and Auxillius.

Chapter 35

The Slave Returns

The trio headed along the shores of Conaille Muirthemne, which formed the southern part of the Ulidian Kingdom. They steered past an inlet, past the mountains of the southern Dalriada, and came to a small landlocked bay. Patrick rowed into the narrow straight, the sea portal to Strangford Lough, in the district of Magh-Inis. They landed the boat on the southern shore of the bay at the mouth of the Slan stream. Hiding the boat, the men journeyed over land, northwest to Dalriada.

Patrick continued until he saw once more the slopes of Mount Slemish looming in the distance. He wanted to pay the ransom price of a slave to his former master, Miliucc. And of course, Patrick desired to share with him the blessings and freedom of God in the gospel.

Odhrain never ceased reminding Miliucc about the prophecy concerning Patrick, and now that Patrick was approaching, Miliucc was driven mad with fear. Seized with terror, he believed his former slave would cast a spell on him and force him to embrace a new religion against his will. Consumed with madness, Milliuc was persuaded by Odhrain to gather all his goods into his house. "It is more honorable to die than be forced into a new religion by a slave!" Milliuc told himself.

Odhrain joined Miliucc in the house with a blazing torch. The flames of the pyre met Patrick's eyes as he stood on the southwestern side of Mount Slemish. Patrick stood for hours dumb with surprise and grief.

"Only God knows his heart, this man who gave himself up to the flames to avoid believing and serving the eternal God . . . I do not know, but God knows," was all his friends could manage to hear Patrick say.

Wanting to be alone, Patrick climbed the rocky slopes to the top of Mount Slemish. All kinds of memories came flooding back to him. It was here God had reached into his heart with his grace and filled him with his love. It was here he had spent many long days and nights on his knees, in all kinds of weather, crying out to the Lord in prayer. Once again Patrick poured his heart out to his Savior.

Comforted by spending time with the Lord, Patrick rose and made his way down the mountain. He didn't know why God had allowed Miliucc to die before he heard the gospel. But Patrick didn't have to know. He was content to believe that Milliuc was in the hands of God and that was the best place for him. Patrick's faith had been tested many times to know that man's ways are not always God's ways, but that God's ways are always best.

Patrick sought out Fith and Auxillius and found them speaking to a group of people. Smoke was still billowing up from where Miliucc had burned his house down. People were milling around trying to make sense of what had happened. As he drew nearer, he recognized one of the voices.

"Killian!" Patrick shouted and ran to meet his dear friend.

"Oh, Patrick, it is so good to see you!" Killian said as he embraced his friend. "Fith and Auxillius have been updating me on what the Lord has been doing through you."

"Well, I guess Odhrain is no longer a threat," Patrick mused, looking over at the rubble of smouldering wood.

"Hey, you remember these two fellows, don't you?" Killian asked with a smile.

Patrick couldn't suppress a grin as he saw Aelric and Berach coming toward him.

"Well, look now, Berach," Aelric said in a joking tone. "It's our little holy Roman boy all grown up." Berach laughed shyly.

"How's the leg, Berach?" Patrick asked.

"Been fine ever since," Berach said quietly. "Thanks to you," he added and took Patrick's hand. Patrick could see tears welling up in Berach's eyes.

"Aelric and Berach have joined our little church, Patrick," Killian informed him. "In fact, there is someone else who you will be surprised to know has joined the faith."

Patrick and the others followed Killian toward what was left of the rath. A shocked and meager group of people were huddled together. A familiar looking tall, muscular man with flowing black hair, now streaked with grey, stood in the middle of them. He seemed to be talking to the people. As Patrick drew closer, he caught a glimpse of gold on the man's right arm flashing in the sunlight.

The man turned as Patrick and his companions approached. Patrick's heart leapt as he silently mouthed the man's name, "Gosact."

Gosact walked briskly over to Patrick and knelt on the ground before him with his head bowed. "Patrick, I am sorry for everything I have done to you, for how I treated you. Will you please forgive me?" Gosact wept.

Overtaken with emotion, Patrick knelt beside Gosact and put his hand on his quaking shoulder. "I forgive you, Gosact." He could not believe this was happening. But, yes, he could! As he knelt beside Gosact he remembered all the times he sat chained to the whipping post being flogged by a raging Gosact. He remembered how much he had hated him, but he also remembered how many times he had prayed for him. When God had changed his heart, he had put a love and concern in his heart for Gosact's soul.

"Gosact," Patrick said softly and warmly, "God has forgiven me much. I forgive you." Gosact clung to Patrick. Their tears turned to tears of joy as they embraced each other as brothers.

Killian spoke to those near. "This is the power and grace of our Almighty Heavenly Father. The power to change a hard sinner's heart and the grace to forgive someone who has behaved so sinful against you."

Patrick, with great pleasure, officially instituted the church at Fochlad. This small gathering of believers had grown to consist of most of the tuath now. Patrick also ordained Killian as its priest.

"Killian, I have a gift for you," Patrick said to his friend.

Killian took a large parcel from Patrick's hands and uncovered it from the cloth that was wrapped around it.

"Oh, Patrick, thank you!" Killian said in awe as he beheld a Bible in his grasp. "I can't believe it," he said. "The very words of God!"

"Remember when I was going to try and steal parchment from Odhrain?" Patrick asked, chuckling.

"Yes," Killian laughed. "You were always up to something!"

Patrick spent a few weeks with Killian in the Braid Valley. He tutored Killian in reading so that he could better read the Bible to his congregation. Killian worked hard and had remembered a great deal from when Patrick had taught him a little when he was a slave. Fith and Auxillius helped the people rebuild their rath. And along with Patrick, they helped Killian teach them from the scriptures the things of God.

Gosact was now chief of the tuath. Patrick was amazed to learn how Gosact had come to trust in Christ. The witness of Killian and the other Christian slaves had begun to perplex Gosact's mind. Odhrain's constant reminding of Patrick and the prophecy kept haunting him. Gosact saw the difference in the behavior of the Christian slaves with that of Odhrain and himself. He couldn't get over how these Christians kept praying for him and were so kind to him when he was so cruel to them. All these things finally persuaded Gosact to seek the one true God. He found himself hiding close to where Killian and his worshippers would have their services, just as Patrick had done. Gosact became convicted of his sin and believed in Christ as his Savior.

Gosact tried to persuade his father in the end to heed Patrick when he came. But Miliucc would not hear of it. Miliucc's mind had gone mad with fear and would not listen. He would only listen to Odhrain. Odhrain had even managed to poison Miliucc against his own son.

Such is the love of God, that two people who were bitter enemies found themselves standing together, arm in arm, at the wooden gate through which Patrick had once snuck quietly away in the middle of the night.

"Farewell, Gosact," Patrick said. "My prayers are with you."

"Godspeed, Patrick. The Lord is with you. You know you will always have a home here," Gosact replied.

Chapter 36

Bonfire at Slane

Patrick and company journeyed in silence for a good while. "Where do you have in mind to go now?" Fith asked Patrick as they walked.

"I sense that the Lord wants us to go to the land of Connaught, to the High King at Tara," said Patrick. "If it is the Lord's will to save King Loaghaire, then he will grant us the freedom to establish churches all throughout Ireland. We will give the gospel to those we find along the way." Alone with his thoughts again, Patrick marvelled at how Lupita was daughter in law to the High King of Ireland. And Loaghaire was the son of High King Niall who had ordered the raid in which he was kidnapped years ago! God's sovereignty is so amazing!

The missionary band kept travelling inland now, having left their boat long ago with Lomman. Fith sang jubilantly from the Psalms. "The Lord has been so good and has answered our prayers, hasn't he, Patrick?"

"Yes, he has indeed," Patrick replied. "But remember, Fith and Auxillius, it will not always be this easy. There will come times of trial."

"But the Lord will always be with us," Auxillius stated.

"The Lord will be with us through everything," said Patrick. "Even the hard times."

The sun was just beginning to set as the trio came upon a small rath owned by a chieftain by the name of Secsnen. "We will try and find rest here," Patrick said.

The missionaries were warmly welcomed into the rath. "Your fame is spreading, Patrick," Secsnen said to his guest. "We will hear for ourselves whether the prophecy about you is true."

Benen, son of the chief, was captivated by Patrick. He could not take his eyes off this stranger. He was so meek but spoke with such authority. Listening to Patrick give the gospel made him truly believe that he spoke the words of eternal life.

When Patrick and his companions set out the next morning Benen begged Patrick to let him go with them. "We could use more help," Patrick looked at Secsnen. Secsnen gave his son permission.

"It is almost Easter," Patrick said to his friends. "There is an ancient festival at Tara that the High King will be celebrating. The chieftains of Ireland will be summoned to celebrate the feast." With a twinkle in his eye, Patrick picked up his blackthorn staff and headed out of the rath. "If the Lord wills, we will hopefully be able to strike a blow against the druids who hold control over the chieftains. Then we will secure freedom to preach the gospel throughout all Ireland."

High King Laoghaire sat regally on his chair with Machra and Lochru, his two best druids, on either side of him. An ancient scroll was laid out on the oak table before them.

> "HE SHALL COME, WITH HIS CROOKED
> HEADED STAFF AND ROBE. HE SHALL
> CHANT BLASPHEMY FROM HIS TABLE,
> AND ALL HIS HOUSEHOLD SHALL
> ANSWER HIM: SO BE IT, SO BE IT. WHEN
> ALL THIS HAPPENS, OUR KINGDOM
> SHALL NOT STAND."

Lochru read the words while his bony finger pointed along the parchment.

"This prophecy is coming close to being fulfilled," Machra warned. "If you are not careful, your reign will come to an end," the druid whispered in a raspy voice to Laoghaire.

"Yes," Lochru hissed in agreement. "You need to deal with this Patrick once and for all. His Christianity is taking root across the land. You need to put an end to him."

"The prophecy clearly points to this man Patrick," Machra added. "He will destroy all our gods and our way of life. Our oracles have announced this for a very long time. He will seduce our people and overthrow our kings."

King Laoghaire slammed his fist down on the table. "Enough! All the chiefs and druids will be here tomorrow. The druids can muster all their strength to defy this Patrick and overcome him."

The king stood up. "Send out the decree that tomorrow all fires throughout the kingdom be extinguished until the signal blaze is kindled in the royal hall," Laoghaire ordered, following the custom that no fire should be lit until one had been kindled in the royal house.

The following morning, Laoghaire followed his druids to the outdoor altar in front of the temple. The altar was adorned with freshly cut daffodils, tulips, crocuses, and green leaves, the fruits of spring. He had not slept well during the night. Breathing in the cool, damp air, the king took in the changing of the seasons. Looking out over the darkness, he strained his eyes in a vain search for this disturber of his kingdom. The waning moon cast eerie shadows on the ground.

The festival of Ostara was about to begin. High King Laoghaire waited anxiously with his druids for the sun to start its ritual climb in the sky. This was a time of balance, of equal light and dark. Then the great bonfire would be lit and would be seen for many miles in every direction.

Machra started chanting, "The sun draws ever closer to us,

greeting the earth with its welcoming rays. Light and dark are equal, and the sky fills with light and warmth." The black and grey shadows started to fade away as the sun's rays dispelled the darkness. Color started to appear as the sun rose higher.

Lochru continued the chanting, "Spring has come! For this we are thankful! The Divine is present all around. Welcome life! Welcome light! Welcome spring!"

Laoghaire could feel the cool earth beneath his feet and the warm sun on his face. Machra was poised with his torch in hand, ready to light the sacred fire. The king paused for a moment and looked out over the countryside for one last glimpse. The early morning mist was beginning to clear and Laoghaire could now see far into the distance. What caught his eye made his blood start to boil. To the north, across the plain of Breg, on top of the Hill of Slane, a fire was blazing for all to see!

Knowing that his fire would soon reach the eyes of the High King, Patrick and his companions got down on their knees in prayer. They prayed for the Holy Spirit's protection, for strength, and for Christ to be victorious. They prayed for Laoghaire's soul.

"Take heart, brothers," Patrick encouraged Fith, Auxillius, and Benen.

"There are only three of us," Auxillius spoke in an anxious voice, trying hard to hide how frightened he was.

Patrick looked at his three friends. "Yes, but God is with us! He will fight for us!"

"We must destroy the one who has defied you!" Lochru shouted with rage. Laoghaire was livid.

"O, King, live forever! This fire, which has been lit in defiance of your royal edict, will blaze forever in this land unless it is extinguished this very day. And the one who kindled it and the kingdom that he speaks of will overpower us all. It will spread over all the country and will reign forever and ever!"

"Come, we will go put this reviler to death and put an end to this prophecy!" Laoghaire stormed to the stables.

Chariots were prepared, and together with his druids and warriors, Laoghaire set out to the Hill of Slane.

"Drive contrary to the sun's course!" Lochru instructed the charioteers. "Our powers need to be built up."

They came to the Hill of Slane, rising just above the left bank of the River Boyne. It was all the druids could do to keep the king from running at Patrick with his spear.

"Do not go up to meet him! He might seduce you with his powers," Mathra said. "He will try and make you worship his God. Who knows what spells he has put into such a fire?"

Laoghaire reluctantly agreed to meet Patrick at a safe distance from the fire. As Patrick approached, the king ordered that no one of his company was to show any sign of respect to this man.

"Lay hands on him!" King Laoghaire shouted as Patrick approached.

When Patrick saw the chariots and horses he shouted out, "Some may trust in chariots, and some in horses, but we trust in the name of the Lord our God."

The druids put forth all their strength and employed all their spells to try and destroy Patrick. Patrick and his companions countered the druids with prayers to Almighty God.

Suddenly a great darkness fell, casting all in an eerie shadow. The ground began to quake, causing men to stumble and fall. Deafening cries were let out by the horses as the earthquake overthrew the chariots.

In the tumult the druids fell on each other. Horses and men fled over the plain in all directions. One of Laoghaire's warriors fell to the ground dead, his skull striking a stone.

Patrick found his feet again as the earthquake subsided. He helped Fith, Auxillius, and Benen to stand, glad to find they were unhurt.

"I curse you!" High King Laoghaire shouted. The High King continued his threats as one of his warriors grabbed him by the arm and forced him into a recovered chariot. "I will destroy you!" he continued ranting on in fury, cursing at Patrick as he drove away to Tara.

Fith, Auxillius, and Benen came up beside their leader. "Let God arise and let his enemies be scattered. Let those that hate him flee before him," Patrick commented.

Back at Tara the queen tried in vain to console her husband. Lochru came and stood beside them and shuddered with fear. "The prophecy is fulfilled. The fire will never be put out." Across the valley Patrick's fire blazed on mightily.

Chapter 37

Queen Angias

E arly the next morning Laoghaire's queen lay in bed watching her husband toss and turn next to her in a fitful sleep. She slipped out quietly, careful not to waken the king. She grabbed a long, woolen cloak and pulled it snug over her shoulders, fastening it at her chin. Then, taking one more glance at her husband, the queen tiptoed across the floor and out the door.

Taking cover behind huts and carts, the queen kept to the early dawn shadows as she made her way to the stables. She pulled her hood well over her head so that no early risers would recognize her.

The horses were quiet as the queen entered the dark stables and made her way down the rows of stalls. Stopping in front of her favorite mare's stall, she took an apple out from her cloak, quietly opened the latch and slipped inside. The jet - black mare lifted her head to nudge the queen and let out a low grunt.

"Sshhh," the queen whispered. "Yes, I brought you something." She held out the apple and the mare took the fruit gratefully and was happy to be led out of her stall. The queen led the mare out of the stables, sticking close to the outer walls. Then she swiftly mounted her mare and took off down the path that led down from Tara to the Plain of Breg.

Patrick met the morning on his knees in prayer. It was Easter morning. He woke before dawn and praised his heavenly Father for raising Christ his Savior from the dead, securing salvation and the forgiveness of sins for his people.

Fith, Auxillius, and Benen were still asleep. Yesterday's events had taken a lot out of the three young men. Patrick stoked the fire with a stick, and he felt a rush of warmth from the flames, the same fire that had caused such a ruckus the day before. The enormous bonfire had burned down considerably. The red flames gave off a glow of patterns that danced on Patrick's face.

Patrick thought he heard a horse whinny and turned around. He could barely make out a figure on a horse approaching his camp.

"Fith, Auxillius, Benen, wake up," Patrick called over to where his companions lay stretched out on the ground. "We have company."

The dark figure dismounted and started walking cautiously in Patrick's direction. She stopped a few yards from the missionaries' camp.

"We mean you no harm," Patrick called out. His companions were standing now at his side, alert and ready to come to their leader's aid.

The mare pawed and stomped the ground nervously while tugging on the rope, trying to get away from the queen's grasp.

"We will not hurt you or your horse," Patrick called out again. "Please know that we are here in peace." Patrick took a few steps closer to the queen, stretching out his arm towards the mare. He kept his eyes locked with the mare's eyes and stroked her nuzzle, calming her down.

"You have a way with animals," the secret visitor said as she pulled her hood off her head. She looked at Patrick with curious but cautious and cunning eyes.

"Queen Angias," Patrick acknowledged the woman before him. "Why are you here?"

The queen looked intently at Patrick. She also stole glances at the fire that still burned bright in defiance of her husband's rule.

"I know you are a mighty and just man," Angias replied stoically. "I beg you to not destroy the king. He will worship your God. I will see to it. Just don't destroy him," she pleaded.

"I have not come here to destroy anyone," Patrick said with compassion in his voice. "It is my desire that your husband comes to know and love the one true God. You see, Angias, God the Father longs to draw you and Loaghaire to himself, to love you and give you everlasting life."

As Patrick spoke these words to the Queen, she felt her heart soften at his warmth and concern. Then remembering who she was she regained her stoic composure. "Come to the High Hall at Tara today. King Laoghaire will bow his knee to your God." She swiftly mounted her mare and sped across the plain.

Patrick and his companions watched Queen Angias gallop away. "Come, friends, we have much praying to do before we can go to meet the king," Patrick resolved. "This is another opportunity the Lord has given us."

Back at Tara, King Laoghaire sat at the long, wooden table, not able to eat his breakfast. Rage mixed with fear was turning his stomach inside out and making his blood boil. "I can't believe you invited that defiler to come here!" Laoghaire shouted at his queen. "And to share my feast!"

"Don't you see, husband?" Angias implored. "Just pretend to give allegiance to his God. Then all you have to do is devise a way to have him killed while he is here."

"She is right," Lochru agreed. "You may have been given another chance to spare the kingdom from this man. This will be the only way."

Chapter 38

Fire Aflame!

King Laoghaire walked through the standing stones on top of a mound to the north of the High Hall. The large stone representing Cernunnos towered above him. He thought of his father, Niall, who was known as "Niall of the Nine Hostages." Niall had once held hostages from all the provinces of Ireland and from Britain. His remembered how his father looked on with pride when he had driven his chariot successfully between the standing stones as fast as he could, proving that he was the rightful heir to the throne.

Laoghaire looked with reverence upon the Lia Fail, Stone of Destiny, standing high on top of the ancient hill called the King's Seat. The stone was brought to Tara by the godlike people, the Tuatha De Danann, as one of their sacred objects. It was used as a coronation stone to crown the high kings of Ireland. The druids said that according to their legends it would roar when it was touched by the rightful king of Tara, its screams heard all over Ireland.

All this power and honor was his. The gods had bestowed authority and power upon Laoghaire, just as they had on his father

Niall, and upon all his fathers before him. It was his right to rule. He was not going to let some stranger walk in and take it all away.

Patrick and his friends made their way to Tara. The Plain of Breg was getting a lot of activity from travelers these last few days.

"He could have us all killed," Fith admitted with a worried voice.

"King Laoghaire does intend to kill me," Patrick replied calmly.

They walked along in silence for a few long moments until Auxillius broke in. "Why are you never afraid, Patrick?"

"There are many times I have been afraid. But my confidence in God far outweighs my fears. God has never promised to keep me from trouble, but he has promised to be with me through everything."

Fith, Auxillius, and Benen did not have to ask Patrick how he had this complete confidence in God. Living with this man of God and striving with him for the gospel, these three men saw in their teacher a life lived bathed in prayer. They had seen him come through the most horrendous trials with a calm and steady trust and confidence only because Patrick stayed in constant communion with his heavenly Father.

"Throw yourselves into God's hands, brothers," Patrick went on. "He reigns over all things. And he gives us the promise of heaven!"

King Laoghaire anxiously waited for the arrival of Patrick. "Is it ready?" he asked Mathra.

The druid held out a golden goblet of wine in his bony hand. "I prepared it myself, O king." The poison swirled unseen, mingling with the red wine. "I will place it at the reviler's seat with my own hand." The two men walked through the heavy oaken doors and into the festivities in the banqueting hall.

A musician was plucking a tune from a harp while a bard sang a melodious epic from Irish history. Tables were piled with meats, cheeses, and bread. Servants filled wine goblets. The hall was filled with revelry. Queen Angias was sitting, adorned in her royal robes, pretending to enjoy the merrymaking.

Laoghaire sat down beside his wife while Mathra placed the poisoned drink at the place designated for Patrick. As Angias placed an assuring hand upon her husband's arm, the entrance doors to the hall were swung open.

"Patrick of Britain is here!" a servant shouted, proclaiming Patrick's arrival.

All the music and noise stopped as Patrick and his companions walked through the entrance and into the hall. Laoghaire and Angias rose from their seats, along with Lochru and Mathra, and walked over to greet their guests. Everyone in the hall kept silent as they eyed the visitors suspiciously.

"Welcome to the feast of Tara, and to my hall," Laoghaire boomed. "It is an honor to have you here."

"Thank you, King Laoghaire," replied Patrick. "We come here today to proclaim to you and your house that on this Easter Day the Lord Jesus Christ has risen from the dead and desires to grant salvation to those who would believe."

Now all eyes were on the High King, curious how Laoghaire would respond. "Before the feasting begins, I wish to bow my knee to your God, in the sight of all my people. I will let them see that King Laoghaire of Tara worships your God as well."

With great flamboyance, Laoghaire prostrated himself before Patrick and grabbed onto his staff. "I, High King Laoghaire, choose to worship this God of Patrick."

Patrick took the king's arm. "Only God knows your heart. It is my prayer that you come to know and love the one true God personally, not as my God, but as yours as well."

Laoghaire looked at Patrick, not comprehending his words. Greed and power overtaking him, and with murder in his heart, he beckoned for Patrick and his friends to come to the table. When all the chieftains were assembled at their seats the king gave the order for the feasting to begin. The musicians took up their instruments and started playing again. The din of revelry quickly came back to the hall.

The king and his druids kept their eyes glued on Patrick as he ate and drank. With each sip that Patrick took from his cup, Laoghaire's face became redder and redder. "Why will he not die?" Laoghaire asked Mathra, his voice seething with anger.

"Let me try and break him," Lochru asked the king. He stood up and addressed Patrick. "Let us go out and work some miracles. We will show who is more powerful."

Patrick replied, "Only God can work miracles. I will not work anything against the will of God. It is God who works through me. You can work only evil, but not good."

"If you can't kill him, you must learn his powers," Angias whispered to her husband. "Get him on your side. His powers combined with yours will give you even greater control over the kingdom."

The king turned to Patrick, the anger and rage replaced with defeat. "I will grant you permission and safety to travel throughout my kingdom, and to speak of this one true God."

Laoghaire slumped in his chair, exhausted. Dubtach, the chief bard, stood and with his melodious voice began singing a tale of the druidical prophecy being fulfilled. The sacred fire of the gospel, kindled by Patrick, would now blaze across the land, never to be put out.

Afterword

Patrick sat at his desk with his hands clasped together. As he had done a million times before, his head was bowed but his heart was lifted to heaven in prayer. His old body would not allow him to go up on the mountain and brave the cold, rain, and wind anymore. But still he cried out to his Heavenly Father. His face radiated with the love and joy of the Son of God.

Laying on his desk was a parchment with the title "Confession" inscribed on the top. Patrick picked his Confession up and held it to the light. "Thank you, Lord, for giving me the words to write," he prayed.

Smiling with satisfaction, Patrick sighed as he read over the document. He praised God as he reminisced about the various events of his life, now recorded as a testimony to the glory of God. Patrick praised God for giving him a mother and grandfather who knew the Lord and taught him Scripture. He thanked God for using Irish raiders to kidnap him and take him to a place where he would be stripped of self and confronted with his sin. He blessed the Lord for how he poured his love and grace into his heart and saved his soul. He praised God for filling him with the Holy Spirit and for the sweet communion he enjoyed with the Lord in prayer. He gratefully expressed praise to God for calling him to share Christ and preach the gospel to the people of Ireland. And he wondrously thanked his heavenly Father for the many thousands of people who were converted and baptized in the name of the Lord Jesus Christ.

"Oh God my Father, may this bring glory to you alone," Patrick prayed. He folded the Confession, sealed it with red wax, and laid it down on his desk.

Patrick died and went to be with his Lord and Savior Jesus Christ on the 17th March, 461 A.D. in Saul, where he had planted his first church in Ireland.